The Essential Commandment

A DISCIPLE'S GUIDE TO
LOVING GOD AND OTHERS

Greg Ogden

IVP Connect

An imprint of InterVarsity Press
Downers Grove, Illinois

InterVarsity Press
P.O. Box 1400, Downers Grove, IL 60515-1426
World Wide Web: www.ivpress.com
Email: email@ivpress.com

InterVarsity Press® is the book-publishing division of InterVarsity Christian Fellowship/USA®, a movement of students and faculty active on campus at hundreds of universities, colleges and schools of nursing in the United States of America, and a member movement of the International Fellowship of Evangelical Students. For information about local and regional activities, write Public Relations Dept., InterVarsity Christian Fellowship/USA, 6400 Schroeder Rd., P.O. Box 7895, Madison, WI 53707-7895, or visit the IVCF website at <www.intervarsity.org>.

All Scripture quotations, unless otherwise indicated, are taken from the Holy Bible, New International Version®. NIV®. *Copyright ©1973, 1978, 1984 by International Bible Society. Used by permission of Zondervan Publishing House. All rights reserved.*

While all stories in this book are true, some names and identifying information in this book have been changed to protect the privacy of the individuals involved.

Design: Cindy Kiple
Images: ©Royce DeGrie/iStockphoto

ISBN 978-0-8308-1088-8

Printed in the United States of America ∞

Library of Congress Cataloging-in-Publication Data

Ogden, Greg.
  The essential commandment: a disciple's guide to loving God and others/Greg Ogden.
    p. cm.
  Includes bibliographical references.
  ISBN 978-0-8308-1088-8 (pbk.: alk. paper)
  1. Love—Biblical teaching—Textbooks. 2. God—Worship and love—Biblical teaching—Textbooks. 3. Christian life—Biblical teaching—Textbooks. I. Title.
  BS680.L64033 2012
  241'.677—dc23

                                                                    2011023114

| P | 23 | 22 | 21 | 20 | 19 | 18 | 17 | 16 | 15 | 14 | 13 | 12 | 11 | 10 | 9 | 8 | 7 | 6 | 5 |
| Y | 31 | 30 | 29 | 28 | 27 | 26 | 25 | 24 | 23 | 22 | 21 | 20 | 19 | 18 | 17 | | | | | |

Contents

Getting the Most from *The Essential Commandment* 7

Introduction: Jesus Believes It Is Possible! 13

  1 The Essential Commandment Explained 21

PART ONE: LOVE THE LORD YOUR GOD . . . WITH ALL YOUR HEART 33

  2 A Broken and Contrite Heart 35

  3 A Listening Heart 49

PART TWO: LOVE THE LORD YOUR GOD . . . WITH ALL YOUR SOUL 61

  4 A Soul That Thirsts for God 63

  5 A Soul . . . Fully Alive . . . to the Glory of God 75

PART THREE: LOVE THE LORD YOUR GOD . . . WITH ALL YOUR MIND . . . 89

  6 Having the Mind of Christ 91

  7 Transformation of the Mind 105

PART FOUR: LOVE THE LORD YOUR GOD . . . WITH ALL YOUR STRENGTH . 121

  8 Focusing Our Energy 123

  9 Growing Healthy Bodies 138

PART FIVE: LOVE YOUR NEIGHBOR AS YOURSELF 153

  10 Have Mercy for Those in Need 155

  11 Love Those Who Would Do You Harm 169

  12 Demonstrate Compassion: Love's Evidence 184

Appendix A: How Are We to Understand the Essential Commandment? 197

Appendix B: Building a Discipleship Ministry 200

Getting the Most from
The Essential Commandment

What would happen to the church of Jesus Christ if a majority of those who claim to follow Christ were nurtured to maturity through intimate, accountable relationships centered on the essentials of God's Word? Self-initiating, reproducing disciples of Jesus would be the result.

The Essential Commandment is specifically designed to implement small, reproducible discipleship units. The vision that stands behind this tool is an ever-expanding, multi-generational discipling network. This tool brings together three conditions which create the climate for the Holy Spirit to bring about accelerated growth.

The first condition for transformation is the unchanging truth of God's Word. We have moved into a post-Christian era in the Western world. Previously, when Christendom reigned, it was generally assumed that there was such a thing as a "revealed" truth or at least scientific, objective truth that was true for all. But now in these post-Christian times relativism prevails, especially in the realm of morals and lifestyles. "Live and let live" is the byword that reflects today's highest value—*tolerance*. It is assumed that all lifestyles and moral convictions are equal, because all truth is personal. In the midst of this morass of relativism, each of these twelve chapters is built around a "core truth" that is true for all, because the source of this truth is a God who is the same for all.

For the truth of God's Word to be released in its transforming power, though, it must be pursued in the context of trusting, intimate and lasting relationships.

The second condition for spiritual transformation in the Holy Spirit's laboratory is trans-parent relationships. The individual has replaced the family or community as the basic unit of our society. Serial and discarded relationships mark our era. The prevailing philosophy is personal fulfillment based upon what feels good or right for me now. Many have not even witnessed the health of long-term, loving commitment. At the core of every human being is the desire for deep and satisfying relationships because we are created in the image of God. God made us for relationship with himself and with one another. A small discipleship group is a place to learn how to be intimate and self-revealing in a safe place over time. What we will ultimately have when all is said and done is the people we love.

Transformation occurs when we grapple with the truth of God's Word in the context of transparent relationships. It is a biblical axiom that the Holy Spirit will have free sway in our lives to the extent to which we open ourselves up to one another. Honesty with God is not sufficient. We give God permission to reshape our lives when we risk self-revelation and confession to others. We can't grow in Christ by ourselves. We are people made for community.

The third condition for transformation is mutual accountability. Accountability is taking the relational context of discipleship to another level. Accountability means giving your discipling partners authority to call you to keep the commitments you have made to one another. You will convene your discipling relationship around a mutual covenant (see p. 12). A covenant is a shared agreement whereby you clearly state your mutual expectations. In so doing you are giving each other permission to hold you to your agreement.

In summary, when the truth of God's Word is at the heart of self-revealing, intimate relationships rooted in mutual accountability, you have the necessary elements for Spirit-motivated transformation. This tool provides the structure for these three elements to come together. Add to this discipling unit a vision for equipping followers of Jesus to pass on the faith from one generation to the next, and you have the components to renew a ministry from the bottom up.

CONTEXTS FOR DISCIPLING

Discipling in the minds of many has become associated with a one-on-one, teacher-student relationship. When I wrote *Discipleship Essentials,* I experimented with the material in a number of contexts. Up to that point my discipling paradigm had also been one-on-one. In addition to this traditional approach I led a threesome called a *triad* and a discipleship group of ten. I was startled by the difference in dynamics. I have come to see groups of three or four as the optimum setting for making disciples.

Why do I believe that a triad or quad is superior to one-on-one? (1) The one-on-one sets up a teacher-student dynamic. The pressure is on the discipler to be the answer person or the fountain of all wisdom and insight. When a third person is added, the dynamic shifts to a group process. The discipler can more naturally make his or her contribution in the dynamic of group interchange. (2) Triad discipling shifts the model from hierarchical to relational. The greatest factor inhibiting those who are being discipled to disciple others (multiplication) is the dependency fostered by one-on-one relationships. The triad/quad, on the other hand, views discipleship as a come-alongside relationship of mutual journey toward maturity in Christ. The hierarchical dimension is minimized. (3) The most startling difference between one-on-one and threes or fours is the sense of "groupness." The sense of the Holy Spirit's being present in our midst occurred much more often in the group versus the one-on-one. (4) There is wisdom in numbers. The group approach multiplies the perspectives on Scripture and application to life issues, whereas one-on-one limits the models and experience. By adding at least a third person there is another perspective brought to the learning process. The group members serve as teachers of one another. (5) Finally, and not to be minimized, by adding a third or fourth person who is being equipped to disciple others, the multiplication process is geometrically increased.

You might ask, if three is better than two, why isn't ten better than three? The larger the group, the more you water down the essential elements that make for transformation. (1) *Truth*—Learning occurs in direct proportion to the ability to interact with the truth, which becomes more difficult with an increased number of voices contributing. It also becomes increasingly difficult to tailor the rate of learning to the individual, the larger the size of the group. (2) *Transparent relationships*—Self-disclosure is integral to transformation, and openness becomes increasingly difficult in direct proportion to the size of the group. If we are not free to divulge our struggles, then the Spirit will not be able to use the group members to effectively minister at the point of need. (3) *Mutual accountability*— The larger the group, the easier it is to hide. Accountability requires the ability to check to see if assignments were completed, or commitments to obedience were maintained. Greater numbers decrease access to a person's life.

ROLE OF THE DISCIPLER

The Essential Commandment can be used in a number of contexts (personal study, one-on-one, one-with-two or a discipleship group of ten), but whatever the context the key person is the discipler. Tools don't make disciples. God works through disciples to model life in Christ for those who desire maturity. Simply covering the content violates the intent of this tool. The tool is a vehicle which helps create the context and provide content for disciplers who want to invest themselves in love and commitment to growing disciples. The tool raises the issues of discipleship, but the discipler embodies the principles in life patterns and convictions. Modeling will be where the real instruction occurs. Remember Jesus' words, "Every one when he is fully taught will be *like* his teacher" (Luke 6:40 RSV).

Studies in secular education reveal that modeling is still the most significant learning dynamic. Neither coercion nor rewards shape human behavior as much as a "motivated attempt to resemble a specific person."[1] The lowest level of learning is compliance when one individual has control over another. The second level is identification. Influence is maintained because of a desire to remain in a satisfying relationship. Internalization is the third and highest step, for the desired behavior has become intrinsically rewarding. Modeling creates an atmosphere that affects values, attitudes and behavior. Some of the specific roles a discipler will carry out are as follows:

1. The first and key role of the discipler is to issue an "invitation to accountable relationship." The commitment is described and the covenant is signed (see p. 12 for "A Disciple's Covenant"). The discipler becomes the "keeper of the covenant." The discipling process should not commence until the invited disciple has prayed over and signed the covenant of commitment. Without the covenant there are no mutually agreed-upon standards for accountability.

2. Initially, the discipler is the group convener and guide. The lessons are laid out in such a way that the discipler simply walks the partners through the discussion format. Approximately one-quarter to one-third of the way through the discipling process, the members rotate the task of guiding the weekly format, as a way to equip and prepare for leadership of the next generation.

3. The discipler prepares the assignments of *The Essential Commandment* just as the disciples do. Even though the discipling appointment will be guided by questions asked by the discipler, the guide shares his or her own responses to the discovery questions in the natural flow of conversation.

4. The discipler models transparency by sharing personal struggles, prayer concerns and confession of sin. The discipler does not need to have all the answers to biblical and theological questions. Feel free to say, "I don't know, but I'll try to find the answer" or "Let's research this together." The power of modeling is not dependent upon a false perfectionism. The discipler will gain as much insight into Scripture and the Christian life as those who are being discipled for the first time.

SUGGESTED STUDY FORMAT

Though *The Essential Commandment* is twelve sessions, I would not expect that you could cover the book in twelve weeks. The relationship is always primary. Just plowing through the lessons would violate the spirit of this type of group. Every group will vary in length according to your style of learning, the depth of personal matters you are sharing at any given time and the detours you take to pursue issues raised by the study. Remember that the idea behind a small, tailored discipleship group is to proceed at the pace that is comfortable for the participants. Don't feel obligated to cover every question, but use this book as a menu from which to select, especially if some of the material is familiar and already incorporated in your life.

The assignments are to be completed individually in their entirety prior to the discipling appointment. Each lesson contains discussion guides specifically designed for each of the following elements:

Core Truth—The core truth serves as the nugget around which each lesson is built. The rest of the chapter is designed to further clarify the central focus. Begin each lesson with a review of the core truth's question and answer.

 Memory Verse—When we commit the Bible to memory, God's viewpoint on life slowly becomes ours. The psalmist writes, "I have hidden your word in my heart that I might not sin against you" (Psalm 119:11). This discipline helps us grow to be more like Christ as we are grounded in his truth, encourage other believers with God's Word and share our faith with others. These verses should be reviewed approximately every fourth session.

 Inductive Bible Study—The place to discover reality from the only perspective that counts is the Bible. We are not interested in stowing away truth as if we were simply trying to acquire more knowledge. The object of this Bible study is to encounter reality and then through God's power bring our lives in line with it.

Reading—Each lesson concludes with a teaching printed in the guide. This reading is intended to provide a contemporary discussion of the eternal core truth that will challenge our lifestyle and stimulate our thinking. The follow-up questions will help make the learning concrete.

Weave prayer through all that you do. Begin by acknowledging Christ's presence through the Holy Spirit, and open your lives to what he may desire to do in you. As you deepen your life together through personal sharing, prayer is a response to the burdens you unload or the blessings God gives. Finally, intercede for one another that you can make the changes in thought, word and deed that the Lord has brought to your attention.

---

[1]*The Study of Identification Through Interpersonal Perception,* quoted in Lawrence O. Richards, *A Theology of Christian Education* (Grand Rapids: Zondervan, 1975), p. 83.

A DISCIPLE'S COVENANT

In order to grow toward maturity in Christ and complete *The Essential Commandment,* I commit myself to the following standards:

1. Complete all assignments on a weekly basis prior to my discipleship appointment in order to contribute fully (see "Suggested Study Format").

2. Meet weekly with my discipleship partners for approximately one-and-a-half hours to dialogue over the content of the assignments.

3. Offer myself fully to the Lord with the anticipation that I am entering a time of accelerated transformation during this discipleship period.

4. Contribute to a climate of honesty, trust and personal vulnerability in a spirit of mutual upbuilding.

5. Give serious consideration to continuing the discipling chain by committing myself to invest in at least two other people for the year following the initial completion of *The Essential Commandment.*

Signed _____

Dated _____

(The above commitments are the minimum standards of accountability. Feel free to add any other elements to your covenant.)

Introduction
Jesus Believes It Is Possible!

Would Jesus ask something of us that couldn't be done?

At the center of all the biblical commands and at the very core of "everything I have commanded you" (Matthew 28:20), Jesus declares that we are to love God with everything we've got and love our neighbors in the same way that we cherish ourselves.

Really? Is this possible?

The energy behind the writing of this curriculum comes from an insight that is quite frankly *embarrassing*. It is embarrassing because I should know better. At first, the insight doesn't seem very dramatic. In fact, every time I have shared this personal "revelation" with others I have been sheepishly apologetic. But here is the amazing truth: *Jesus actually thinks we can become like him.* Jesus actually believes that it is possible for frail and deeply flawed human beings to focus our complete affection on God and others.

The key word here for me is *possible*. I had unconsciously given up the possibility of actually doing what Jesus commanded. No, I had never consciously thought or said, "Jesus, I think you're an idealistic dreamer," or "Jesus, you can only expect so much from flawed humanity." I was not even aware that I had dismissed Jesus' belief in me. But what had taken over my spirit in my attempt to be authentic was a focus on where I had fallen short of Jesus' call. In my desire to make sure that I was not deceiving myself about my capacity for sin, I had given up the upside possibility that the character of Jesus could actually take over my life.

THE IMPOSSIBLE POSSIBILITY

Because of this insight, I have come to realize that we need to hold two truths in dynamic tension. On the one hand, we need to be rigorously honest about our shortcomings. Part of what it means to live in the light of Christ is allowing him to shine that light in the hidden regions of our soul. Yet at the same time we need to hold to the compelling vision that this same light illumines our path so that we can live into our potential of being God- and people-lovers. There is a Hasidic saying that advises us to go around with a piece of paper in each pocket, with one piece reading "I am dust and ashes," and the other, "For me the world was created." Yes, we are finite and broken people as well as those who have been redeemed to reflect the Redeemer. Jesus would not ask us to be and do something unless it was possible. We can become the bodily dwelling place of Jesus who lives his life out through us.

The vision that Jesus has placed before us comes in the form of his summary statement as to what our life agenda is to be. In response to one of the "teachers of the law" seeking to know which commandment was most important, Jesus responded with what we have come to call the Great Commandment: "'Love the Lord your God with all your heart and with all your soul and with all your mind and with all your strength.' The second is this: 'Love your neighbor as yourself.' There is no commandment greater than these" (Mark 12:30-31). He didn't follow this up by saying, "I know I'm asking a lot, but do the best you can. I know you'll never fully approximate this high and lofty goal, but it's still worth striving for." No, I added that part myself. In my spirit I washed out the possibility that this could actually be, saying, "I know the guy dwelling in this body all too well. Not a chance that this weak and feeble individual could ever approximate Jesus' expectation."

Yet something uplifting started to happen when my spirit began to rehearse a different message: "Jesus thinks this is possible." I found a new energy released in me. A buoyancy of spirit beckoned me with the thought that I could live more deeply into the possibility of loving God with all my heart, soul, mind and strength, and loving my neighbor as myself. With Jesus, it *is* possible to "love your enemies, [and] do good to those who hate you" (Luke 6:27). It's not just for that rare person who seems to have tapped into a pool of grace that the rest of us have not been able to find.

THE PARADOX

Herein lies the paradox of being a Christ-follower. We need to embrace what appear to be two competing truths about ourselves—our deeply corrupted spirits and our redemption through Christ—if we are to approximate what Jesus believes is our potential as Great Commandment people.

On the one hand, if we are not deeply in touch with our dark side, we will miss the incredible grace that claimed us while we were in full rebellion against God and into our own self-exaltation. Like the alcoholic in a twelve-step program who started down the road to redemption by saying, "We admitted we were powerless over alcohol," the believer has to acknowledge without qualification, "We admit we are powerless over sin." Left to myself, I don't love God or my neighbor; in fact, I hate God, who crowds my autonomy, and I don't really care what happens to my neighbor, as long I am taken care of. Only when we see the extent of how corrupt our spirit is through and through will we rejoice with Paul's words, "But because of his great love for us, God, who is rich in mercy, made us alive with

Christ even when we were dead in transgressions" (Ephesians 2:4-5).

Without an awareness of our need for grace, we will simply turn the Great Commandment into a new law that we attempt to fulfill by our own effort. It's true that this summary commandment of Jesus serves the dual purpose of the law. On the one hand, the apostle Paul tells us that the law was given to show us how far short we fall before the holiness of God (Romans 7:13). It serves its purpose by driving us to our knees. Just try keeping the command to love God and our neighbors in our own strength. We would not survive our own thought life for the next ten minutes. So in our study of the Great Commandment, we want to avoid making Jesus' commandment simply a higher-level law that leads only to enslavement rather than freedom.

On the other hand, we don't want to miss what is implicit in this command. Jesus thinks that living this truth is possible. We walk carefully between the shoals of being in touch with our capacity for self-deception yet at the same time energized by the new capacity that God's grace gives us to become the redeemed people in whom Christ dwells. Dallas Willard says it succinctly: "Grace is opposed to *earning,* not to effort."[1] The apostle Paul helps us with this tension. On the one hand he said of himself, "I am . . . the worst of sinners" (1 Timothy 1:15-16); on the other hand he said that this awareness infused him with an energy and passion fueled by God's grace that sent him across the known world. Here is how Paul brings these two truths together: "For I am the least of the apostles and do not even deserve to be called an apostle, because I persecuted the church of God. But by the grace of God I am what I am, and his grace to me was not without effect. No, I worked harder than all of them—yet not I, but the grace of God that was with me" (1 Corinthians 15:9-10).

What is the relationship then between grace and law? Is the law nullified by grace? Do we not have to concern ourselves with the commandments this side of grace? To echo Paul, "Absolutely not!" (see Galatians 3:21). Dallas Willard states the connection between grace and law: "The presence of the Spirit and of grace is not meant to set the law aside, but to enable conformity to it from an inwardly transformed personality. . . . Law comes with grace in the renewed soul. There is no such thing as grace without law. The law is the structure of the life of grace in the kingdom of God."[2]

Jesus' command to love God with all we've got and to treat our neighbor with the same regard as we do ourselves is meant to bring us to the end of ourselves. When we hear this expectation we're *supposed* to say, "There is no way in the world that in myself I will ever be able to live up to this standard." This realization should cause us to cast ourselves unreservedly on the grace of God and repent of our sin-sick soul. Then we are flooded with the light of God's accepting grace. Our heart of stone is massaged back to life as a heart of flesh that begins to beat within. We find within a new motivation and desire to want to become all that God hopes us to be. Because our inner affections are being transformed to love what God loves, we begin to understand that his yoke is easy and his burden is light. The law we hated now becomes the life we have always wanted.

TRANSFORMATION OF THE WILL

Dallas Willard was again the one who led me to this breakthrough. In his very helpful article "Spiritual Formation: What It Is, and How It Is Done,"[3] he writes that to be fully formed in Christ is to come to that place where our natural impulses come to reflect the feelings, thinking and actions of Jesus himself. Since the will is the primary locus of this formation—the executive center of our being—Willard speaks of three dimensions or conditions of the will (he equates the will and the heart as we'll see more fully later). He calls the first dimension of the will the *impulsive will:* it's "directed or moved by or toward things that are simply attractive." This is where a baby begins. Babies are simply drawn to what is enticing in their environment. Adults who don't outgrow this impulse to simply do what is pleasing to them are driven by immediacy and enslaved by their own desires.

This appears to be the cultural norm. Robert Bellah and a team of fellow sociologists went in search of the distinguishing characteristics of Americans and then published the results in their classic work *Habits of the Heart.* They found one quality that sets Americans apart from those of other cultures: freedom. But unfortunately it's a rather skewed understanding of freedom; it's the freedom from obligation. This view can be summarized in the following statement: "I want to do what I want to do when I want to do it, and no one better tell me otherwise." Bellah makes the point that this view of freedom as radical independence does not provide the basis for any long-term covenantal relationships such as marriage or even a relationship with God.

Thankfully, Willard identifies a second dimension of the will. As a follower of Christ, he says, a person must adopt the practice of a *reflective will,* which involves beginning to set up a dialogical process where the good that God intends is examined over against our thinking, feeling and acting. In other words, with this type of will we regularly reflect on our life in light of God's revealed truth. For example, almost every day I begin my time of prayer with the ancient spiritual practice of the examen. My simplified version of this prayer is to ask the Lord through his Spirit to take me back through the previous day in order to review what he would have me pay attention to. I call this "praying backwards." My reflective questions are, "Lord, in what way were you present in the interactions and events of the day?" More specifically, "How were you at work? What did I miss? For what can I give thanks?" And then very specifically, "As a result of your life in me, how can I be formed to respond and act more like you?" I both celebrate God's presence and my being in concert with his purposes while also carefully making note of the missed opportunities, misspoken words and other missteps.

While reflection is good, we're not to stop there. The reflective will moves us toward a deeper goal: what Willard calls the *embodied will.* It was while I was reading his insight into this dimension of the will that my "aha" came. Willard, echoing Jesus, says it is possible to become so aligned with Jesus' heart that our automatic responses are simply in tune with God's heart. This is how I apply this to myself: Suppose someone were to come to me and say something like, "I don't get why you want to be a teacher and pastor. You show no evidence of having that gift. What were you thinking when you went into this profession?" Is it possible that the presence of Jesus could so engulf my inner and bodily reactions that my first response would be to want to do good to this person who was insulting me, and to want only the best for their life?

To be formed in Christ is to say, "Yes, it is possible. Yes, this is what I would want my inner world to become. I want to be so in tune with Jesus' life in me that his *embodied will* becomes mine."

CATEGORIES OF CONVICTIONS

In other words, Jesus intends to get down to the very core of our makeup. Michael Novak provides another scheme that parallels Willard's framework of the will. He divides conviction into three categories: public, private and core. John Ortberg picks up on these in his book *Faith and Doubt.*[4]

Public beliefs. Public beliefs are those convictions that *we want other people to think we believe,* even though we may not really believe them. For example, if my wife puts on a dress and asks, "Does this dress make me look like I have wide hips?" the correct answer is, "I didn't even know you had hips."[5] We might express public beliefs in our business life too; for example, there may be politically correct words and phrases that we feel we need to say we believe if we want to be a good company person, but inside we know we don't believe them. Public figures are notorious for uttering public beliefs because they sound good.

The biblical illustration here is King Herod. After Jesus was born, some visitors from the East (whom we call "wise men") told him about the one who was born King of the Jews. Herod told the wise men, "Go and make a careful search for the child. As soon as you find him, report to me, so that I too may go and worship him" (Matthew 2:8). Did King Herod have any intent to worship this child? No, of course not. But it made for good public consumption because it would get him what he wanted.

Private beliefs. Private beliefs are those things *we actually think we believe until they are tested.* For example, on the night before Jesus was crucified, the apostle Peter stated his undying allegiance to Jesus. When Jesus then told Peter that he would deny him before the cock crowed three times, Peter said, "Even if all fall away, I will not. . . . Even if I have to die with you, I will never disown you" (Mark 14: 29, 31).

When Peter said these words, was he sincere in that moment? Did he actually think he believed what he was saying? Yes, I think he did believe. Were these Peter's true convictions? No. When the time came to stand up as a loyal follower of Jesus, he acted like he never knew Jesus.

We never truly know if we believe our convictions until they're tested. We can assert in life or in death that our sure and certain hope is in Jesus Christ, and that nothing can move us off of that foundation. Then we might hear those frightening words, as I did, "You've got cancer!" Only then could I truly look inside myself to see if my sure and certain hope was in Jesus Christ in this life and beyond.

Core beliefs. Our core beliefs are *the convictions that are revealed in our daily actions, based on what we actually do.* These are the mental maps we follow. We will always act out of our core beliefs or convictions, and will never violate them. For example, we believe in gravity. We are not able to violate that belief, so we'll always act with that knowledge in mind. Gravity is part of our mental map. If we want to stay safe, we won't walk to the edge of a hundred-story building; if we want to take our life, we might do so. Our actions are always the result of our core purposes or convictions.

My public convictions, then, are what I want you to think I believe, my private convictions are what I think I believe, but my core convictions are revealed by what I actually do. Where does Jesus target the transformation of our convictions? He intends to change us at our *core beliefs,* to establish his *embedded will* in us. His desire is to be so central and present to us and in us that our automatic responses as well as our intended desire are simply to have our hearts beat next to his.

I am suggesting that this means we live in what might appear at first to be a contradiction, but actually, it's a liberating paradox. On the one hand we must come face to face with our flawed nature and have a sense of how much we must live in grace at all times. There is never a time when we outgrow the need for God's undeserved embrace. As Paul says to his son in the faith, Timothy, "Be strong in the grace that is in Christ Jesus" (2 Timothy 2:1). Whether it's a case of something I've done or something I've failed to do, I need the covering of God's mercy at all times.

Yet . . . God has chosen to put his truth in this clay pot (earthen vessel), which is "being transformed into his likeness with ever-increasing glory, which comes from the Lord, who is the Spirit" (2 Corinthians 3:18). God thinks enough of us to abide in us and then set off on his work of renovation. And Jesus commands us to love God and the ones for whom he laid down his life because he believes that we can actually do it.

The irony is that living into God's possibility is only possible when we confess the impossibility. May the following prayer express the desires of our heart as we begin this journey:

Dear Father, we hear your call to love you with everything that we are and to love those whom you infinitely value. Are you asking us to do something that is not really possible? Part of us confesses that we are only weak creatures whose passion for you can only be described as tepid. We hear that you want us to engage our hearts, souls, minds and bodies in full devotion to you, but when we look at our lives we feel that we pale in comparison to your expectation. If we are going to be what you want us to be, we will need an infusion of love that is not our own. And yet, we so want to live into your belief in us. As we embark on this journey together, create a sense of anticipation in us that you will stretch our capacity beyond what we ever thought was imaginable so that we can live into your possibility for us. Through Jesus Christ we pray, Amen.

---

[1]Dallas Willard, *The Great Omission* (San Francisco: HarperSanFrancisco, 2006), p. 80.
[2]Dallas Willard, *Renovation of the Heart: Putting on the Character of Christ* (Colorado Springs: NavPress, 2002), p. 214.
[3]Dallas Willard <www.dwillard.org/articles/>.
[4]John Ortberg, *Faith and Doubt* (Grand Rapids: Zondervan, 2008), p. 42.
[5]Humor is courtesy of John Ortberg from his teaching "Are You Making Better Christians or More Disciples?" delivered at the 2008 Reveal Conference, Willow Creek Community Church, South Barrington, Illinois. Available through Willow Creek Association resources at <www.willowcreek.com/wca_index.asp>.

1 / The Essential Commandment Explained

Looking Ahead

MEMORY VERSE: Romans 12:1
BIBLE STUDY: 1 John 4:7-21
READING: The Essential Commandment

 **Core Truth**

What should be the focus of our life each day and all of our days?

In response to God's invitation to enter a relationship of covenant love, we are called to return that love to God by placing our full affection on him. So worthy is God of our complete devotion that we are to submit our will (heart), harness our passions (soul), discipline our thinking (mind) and channel our energy (strength) to his glory. As we do so, other people—all cherished by God—will become our priority.

1. Identify key words or phrases in the question and answer above, and state their meaning in your own words.

2. Restate the core truth in your own words.

3. What questions or issues does the core truth raise for you?

Memory Verse Study Guide

In the apostle Paul's masterwork, the book of Romans, he spends the first eleven chapters expounding on the mercy of God across the great sweep of time and eternity. So taken is Paul by this breathtaking picture that he himself has painted that he concludes this section by spontaneously breaking out in doxology, "Oh, the depths of the riches of the wisdom and knowledge of God!" (Romans 11:33). Once this foundation of mercy is laid, Paul then shifts to the implications for how we are to live.

1. *Putting it in context:* Read Romans 11:33–12:2. How does verse 12:1 serve as a transition from Paul's foundational description of mercy to the implications for Christian living?

2. The memory verse is *Romans 12:1*. Copy the verse verbatim.

3. *The Message* by Eugene Peterson is a paraphrase of Scripture that puts it into everyday language. Romans 12:1 in his translation reads, "So here's what I want you to do, God helping you: Take your everyday, ordinary life—your sleeping, eating, going-to-work, and walking-around life—and place it before God as an offering. Embracing what God does for you is the best thing you can do for him." What strikes you about Peterson's rendition of our memory verse?

4. According to Paul, what is the only appropriate response to God's mercy?

5. What do you think it means to be a "living sacrifice"?

6. How does Paul broaden the concept of worship beyond our usual association with a worship service?

7. What parallels do you see between the memory verse and the Essential Commandment* (see Mark 12:29-31)?

---

*Throughout this text the Great Commandment will be referred to as the Essential Commandment in concert with the title of this work.

Inductive Bible Study Guide

The apostle John, in a sense, wrote his own commentary on the Essential Commandment in his first epistle. In it, he tells us that love is at the core of who God is and that this same kind of love is therefore to be reflected through our life.

1. *Read 1 John 4:7-21.* How would you summarize John's line of thought after reading this part of his letter?

2. What is the qualitative nature of the love John describes in verses 7-12?

   How does this shed light on John's claim that "everyone who loves has been born of God"?

3. From what source do we draw this love?

4. What is the connection between love, judgment, fear and punishment according to verses 17-18?

5. Why is it impossible to love God and hate your brother or sister?

6. If you were to do an inventory of your relationships within the body of Christ, where might you find yourself coming up short of John's pointed exhortation in verses 19-21?

Reading: The Essential Commandment

During a visit to Brazil, the late Senator Robert Kennedy was taken to the interior to observe some of the tribal life. Through an interpreter, he was introduced to a native Brazilian who had recently been converted to Christ. Kennedy told the interpreter to ask him what he enjoys doing the most. The native Brazilian's surprising reply was, "Being occupied with God." The senator, expecting the man to say something like fishing or hunting, was convinced that something had been lost in the translation. So he repeated the question, only to hear the same reply: "Being occupied with God."[1]

What an interesting way to speak about our basic pursuit or purpose! I wonder: Would this, in all honesty, even be close to the way we might answer Kennedy's question?

THE BASICS OF LIFE

Jesus reduces life to its raw basics in the Essential Commandment. Hear Dale Bruner's summary: "The purpose of living is the adoration of God and the cherishing of human beings."[2] Unfortunately, we make life far more complicated than this—at least until tragedy strikes. I have vivid memories of walking out of a hospital into the cool of a Southern California evening having just left a waiting room where an extended family had set up camp. They were keeping a prayer vigil, hoping against hope that their nineteen-year-old son/brother/nephew would miraculously recover from a motorcycle accident. In that moment, all they had was hope in God and the love of family and friends. Frankly, nothing else mattered. Job promotions were the farthest thing from their mind. Planning their next vacation hardly mattered. They couldn't have cared less whether they had a new addition on their home or the latest model car. Life had been reduced to the God they loved and the significant people in their life. This family's state of mind may not have been centered on the Essential Commandment, but they certainly reflected its essence.

In the Essential Commandment Jesus not only declares that God's purpose is knowable; he also makes it crystal clear. Jesus simplifies for us the rationale for life. In what we have come to know as the Great Commission, Jesus tells his would-be followers that being his disciple means engaging in a lifetime of obeying "*everything* that I [Jesus] have commanded you" (Matthew 28:20). If we were to enumerate all of Jesus' commands, they could amount to as many as 147 according to one person's calculations.[3] But Jesus has done us a favor in identifying the "greatest" or the "most important" commandment. In the Essential Commandment he takes us to the core of the core.

Life is short, so we have to major on the majors. In the weeks ahead you will get to focus your attention on what Jesus tells us truly counts. We have it on the best authority that the dash between the date of our birth and death should be focused on living the Essential Commandment.

In this initial reading we will explore the account of the Essential Commandment, upon which this book is grounded. This will allow us to establish the framework for the rest of our discoveries.

The question of whether or not there might be such a thing as a "most important" commandment was raised by a teacher of the law who approached Jesus. Impressed with how Jesus had handled a challenge from the Sadducees, he asked, "Of all the commandments, which is the most important?" (Mark 12:28). In Matthew's version, we're told that the Pharisees sent one of their own to test Jesus with the question.[4]

The Pharisees equated righteous living with law keeping. So zealous were they that they had identified 613 laws (248 positive, 365 negative) that must be obeyed, and they considered all of them to be of equal importance. After all, they reasoned, whatever God commands is great no matter how seemingly insignificant. So the question was asked to see if Jesus would elevate some of the commands over others, thereby demonstrating a footloose attitude toward the law. If he did, the Pharisees would then have further "evidence" that Jesus was a law breaker.

Despite the Pharisees' stringent view, in some of the more liberal rabbinic circles it was not uncommon to speak of lighter or weightier laws. Rabbi Hillel,[5] the head of a broad-minded school of thought a generation prior to Jesus' birth, is famous for reducing the entirety of the law to a single sentence. A Gentile promised Hillel the Elder that if he could recite the whole law while standing on one foot, he would convert to Judaism. The rabbi is immortalized for his reply, a negative version of the Golden Rule: "What you yourself hate, do not do to your neighbor: this is the whole law, the rest is commentary. Go and learn."[6]

Jesus weighs in with his summary of the law which takes us to the central purpose of living: "'The most important one,' answered Jesus, 'is this: "Hear, O Israel, the Lord our God, the Lord is one. Love the Lord your God with all your heart and with all your soul and with all your mind and with all your strength." The second is this: "Love your neighbor as yourself." There is no commandment greater than these'" (Mark 12:29-31).

THE SHEMA: HEAR

Jesus introduces the command to "love God and your neighbor" with a quote from Deuteronomy 6:4: "Hear [Shema], O Israel, the LORD our God, the LORD is one." This one loaded sentence is the essence of what is known as the Shema. It would be hard to overstate the significance of the Shema to the identity of God's chosen people. These words appear on the doorpost of almost any Jewish synagogue you might enter.

But why does Jesus introduce the Essential Commandment with these words? The Shema tells us that grace precedes law. A relationship is established in love prior to the expectations that go with it. If we snatch Jesus' summary of the law from this context, it simply becomes an impossible demand; the law is reduced from 613 requirements to 1 massive one. Whether it is many or one, though, God has required what will inevitably end in failure. If this more stringent law is simply intended to serve as a basis for acceptability with God, then we are defeated from the beginning.

But if, in fact, the Essential Commandment is our commitment of obedience to a God who has embraced us in grace, then we are just responding to the mercy extended to us. The Shema contains within it an invitation of grace. It says that the singular God of the universe reached down and claimed a people for himself out of all the peoples on the face of the earth. The Lord took the initiative to enter in a covenant with his people. Grace initiates; grace seeks the object of its love.

Our God is a covenant-making and covenant-keeping God. He is not asking anything of us that he has not already bestowed upon us. Moses captures God's love and pursuit of us in relationship:

> For you are a people holy to the LORD your God. The LORD your God has chosen you out of all the peoples on the face of the earth to be his people, his treasured possession.

The LORD did not set his affection on you and choose you because you were more numerous than other peoples, for you were the fewest of all peoples. But it was because the LORD loved you and kept the oath he swore to your forefathers that he brought you out with a mighty hand and redeemed you from the land of slavery, from the power of Pharaoh king of Egypt. Know therefore that the LORD your God is God; he is the faithful God, keeping his covenant of love to a thousand generations of those who love him and keep his commands. (Deuteronomy 7:6-9)

THE GOD WHO MAKES A COVENANT

The Lord is the covenant-making and covenant-keeping God who enters into a grace-filled relationship with a people he calls his own. Before there was any law, God said, "I will be your God, and you shall be my people" (see Exodus 6:7). The Essential Commandment is therefore the call to respond to a relationship of love that has already been established. It is not a new high bar for us to jump over so that God will be pleased with us. His pleasure in us has already been demonstrated through the life, death and resurrection of Jesus.

In other words, God commits himself to us before we commit ourselves to him.

Images of faithful love mark the covenant-making and covenant-keeping God. Through the prophet Hosea, for example,

God paints a picture of himself as a jilted lover. The Lord instructs Hosea to marry Gomer, a prostitute who rejects exclusive faithfulness to him by giving herself to other suitors, and likens himself to a husband, explaining that he is a jealous God, zealous to reject anyone who diverts the affection of his beloved from him. One of the rich Hebrew words that captures the love of the covenant is *hesed,* which means "loving-kindness, tenderness, faithful devotion."[7] In fact, scholars have noted that the root of *hesed* is related to the word translated "womb," signifying the love of a mother for the fruit of her womb—an apt description of the relationship the Lord has to us, his covenant people.

The Scriptures also reveal God as a father who allows himself to be hurt by his wayward children who fail to recognize the father's tender care. His initial hurt and anger turn to compassion, as Hosea recorded: "How can I give you up, Ephraim? How can I hand you over, Israel? . . . My heart is changed within me; all my compassion is aroused. I will not carry out my fierce anger. . . . For I am God, and not man—the Holy One among you" (Hosea 11:8-9).

Lewis Smedes's words help us understand even more our covenant-keeping God: "Yahweh [the LORD] is the sort that sticks with what he is stuck with."[8] And of course, the entirety of the Old Testament story anticipates Jesus as the revealer of the heart of God. Jesus changes the name of God from "the LORD" to "Abba, Father."

The core of the Christian life, then, is simply to be introduced to our Abba through his Son, who came full of grace and truth.

OUR AFFECTION FOR THE GOD OF THE COVENANT

So what is our response to the covenant-making and covenant-keeping God? We make covenant with him. We enter into an affectionate relationship. We return his love. When we have been loved to the extent demonstrated by our faithful God who lay down his life for us, the only proper response is to show him that same kind of love.

Lewis Smedes says that since God is a promise-making and promise-keeping God, we are most like God when we keep our promises. Our part in the covenant is like the promise that lovers make to each other on their wedding day. A traditional version of the wedding vows is, "I _____, take you, _____, to be my wedded wife (husband), and I do promise and covenant, before God and these witnesses, to be your loving and faithful husband (wife)." Likewise, the Essential Commandment is our response to give exclusive and faithful devotion to the God who has made us for himself.

Scot McKnight says that Jesus essentially turned the Jewish Creed—the Shema—into the Jesus Creed. In his book bearing the title *The Jesus Creed,* McKnight raises the question, How does Jesus have the temerity to take the Shema and add his own twist? Could we, for example, imagine someone taking the Apostles' Creed and adding their own lines to it? You can write you own creed, after all—but you don't mess with something that has been honed through the ages. Yet McKnight says that Jesus does just that to this untouchable creed, adding his own nuances through two additions. First, Jesus connects the love of God inseparably to the love of people by linking Deuteronomy 6:5 to Leviticus 19:18. It is as if Jesus is saying, "If you love God with the totality of your being, it will be evidenced by the way you cherish people." Second, and even more shocking, Jesus makes himself the object of the ultimate love. Consistently throughout his ministry he said in so many words, "Love me with all of your heart, soul, mind and strength."

In essence, Jesus reaffirms Deuteronomy 6:5, which spells out the implications of the Lord being the One God who has bestowed his elective love on the chosen people. We were made from love and for love. Just as God unconditionally committed himself to us, so we in turn are to unreservedly devote all of our faculties toward finding our fulfillment in God. Jesus underscores this totality by the repeated use of the word *all:* "Love the Lord your God with *all* your heart and with *all* your soul and with *all* your mind and with *all* your strength."[9] We generally have taken this to simply mean, "Love the Lord with all you've got. Pull out all the stops." My assumption in writing this book, however,

is that Jesus is intentional about identifying the various faculties—the parts that make up a human being—that we are to engage in our love for him. His detail here is not accidental.

I believe that by examining the elements of what makes us human through the four aspects that Jesus identifies, we can learn to love God with full dedication. To love God is to align our will with his (heart), to marshal our depth of passion (soul), to make him the object of our thought life (mind) and to harness the energy of our bodies (strength). In other words, to love God is to find our joy in the totality of his character and person by bringing the totality of our character and person in concert with him.

Yet Jesus adds to the first command, "The second is this: 'Love your neighbor as yourself.' There is no commandment greater than these" (Mark 12:31). The *Peanuts* cartoonist Charles Schulz put these words in the mouth of blanket-toting Linus: "I love mankind; it's people I can't stand." There is, however, no version of the Essential Commandment that says, "I love God; it's people I can't stand." How could we say that we love God and yet not love who God loves? It is not possible. When we love God we are asking to take on the heart of God, which is manifest in the way we treat those for whom Christ paid the ultimate price.

The journey ahead takes us into the contours and dimensions of what it means to love God and to love our neighbors. We have only one calling or vocation in life. Our calling is to love and be conformed to the image and likeness of Jesus. To paraphrase Mother Teresa, "Our job is not our vocation; becoming like Christ is our vocation. People are confused." When we follow Jesus we naturally fulfill what he said is to be our focus in life. What a joy it is to know what this life is to be all about and to get to spend it in pursuit of its desired intent.

---

[1]Derek Prime, *Created to Praise: Giving God Glory in All of Life* (Downers Grove, Ill.: InterVarsity Press, 1981), p. 26.

[2]Frederick Dale Bruner, *Matthew: A Commentary: The Churchbook, Matthew 13–28* (Dallas: Word, 1990), p. 792.

[3]Compiled and published by the evangelist J. S. McConnell in 1925. Accessed at <www.wowzone.com/commandm .htm>.

[4]For the purposes of this study, we will concentrate on Mark's version of the Essential Commandment.

[5]Renowned within Judaism as a sage and scholar, Rabbi Hillel (c. 110 B.C.–A.D. 10) was the founder of the House of Hillel school for Tannaïm (Sages of the Mishnah).

[6]William Lane, *The Gospel According to Mark,* The New International Commentary on the New Testament (Grand Rapids: Eerdmans, 1974), p. 432.

[7]Norman H. Snaith, *A Theological Word Book of the Bible*, ed. Alan Richardson (New York: Macmillan, 1951), pp. 136-37.

[8]Lewis Smedes, quoted in Scot McKnight, *The Jesus Creed: Loving God, Loving Others* (Brewster, Mass.: Paraclete, 2004), p. 42.

[9]See appendix A, "How Are We to Understand the Great Commandment?"

Reading Study Guide

1. In all honesty, what does your current lifestyle and motivations say about what your purpose in life actually is?

2. The Essential Commandment was Jesus' response to an inquiry about what the "greatest commandment" is. What is the significance of him using the Shema as a preamble to the Essential Commandment?

3. How do we keep the Essential Commandment from becoming just another law that calls us up short and places us under judgment?

4. How does the Essential Commandment become simply our covenantal response to God's covenantal commitment to us?

5. Put into your own words what it means to love God with all of our faculties (heart, soul, mind and strength).

6. In response to the challenge "What is the greatest commandment?" Jesus actually connected two commandments together. How are they inseparable?

7. Take some time to look ahead by examining the contents page. Where do you sense you might face your greatest challenge? Where do you see gaps in your focus?

Going Deeper

Do your own commentary study of this passage to see how reputable scholars look at it. The following suggestions are trustworthy expositions on this core text:

Bruner, Frederick Dale. *Matthew: A Commentary: The Churchbook, Matthew 13–28.* Dallas: Word, 1990.

Lane, William. *The Gospel According to Mark.* The New International Commentary on the New Testament. Grand Rapids: Eerdmans, 1974.

McKnight, Scot. *The Jesus Creed: Loving God, Loving Others.* Brewster, Mass.: Paraclete, 2004.

The key issue to consider is how Jesus' summary of the law does not become just a higher bar that will judge us. You will also want to discuss the introduction to this book, "Jesus Believes It Is Possible." What is the relationship between grace and law?

Part One

LOVE THE LORD YOUR GOD . . .
WITH ALL YOUR HEART

What is the heart? As we will see throughout this study, there is considerable overlap and sometimes interchangeability, particularly when we focus on the heart and soul, in the biblical usage. Biblically, the heart primarily refers to the command center of our being, or our will. God made humans distinct from the rest of living beings in that we can exercise our will (whereas animals are essentially preprogrammed and operate out of instinct). In other words, we are free beings who can choose between alternatives. Life originates in the will. Though we can't speak things into existence out of nothing, as the Lord did, we can imagine or conceive an idea and bring it to reality. In this way, we can *create*—for good or for ill.

The tilt of our heart, the inclination from within, the nature and state of this executive center, will determine the quality of our existence. And it is the state of the heart—the essence of who we are—that God sees and cares about: "Man looks at the outward appearance, but the LORD looks at the heart" (1 Samuel 16:7). Sadly, our wills are fallen and are therefore inclined to rebel against God's authority and distrust his goodness. The sinful will seeks autonomy and freedom without accountability; in our natural state we don't want to be beholden to anyone but ourselves. Our sinful will makes it all about us.

Coming to Christ is therefore a battle of our wills. No one makes a decision to follow Jesus without wrestling. Jesus will only have one place—first. Even once we are "in Christ," there is a constant need to align our will with his desire. To love God with all of our heart is to seek to obey all of his commands and live under his authority.

The two chapters in this section therefore deal with the core issues of how to align our hearts to God's heart and submit our wills to his authority, because to love Jesus is to obey him. Chapter two deals with the biblical theme of a *broken and contrite* heart, which is the kind of heart that is most pliable and moldable in God's hand. If the rebellious heart is described biblically as hard (like a heart of stone) and stiff-necked (highly resistant), then the heart that God can shape is one that is surrendered to the Potter's hand and can therefore be molded like a soft lump of clay.

Chapter three then moves to the heart that is attentive. The heart which produces fruitful character has an ear that is highly attuned to God's voice. In the parable of the sower, Jesus identifies three kinds of soil that inhibit our ability to hear and receive the Word. Then he says that there is a prepared soil that can produce a crop, yielding multiple times the seed sown in the ground. A fruitful heart is a *listening heart*.

2 / A Broken and Contrite Heart

LOOKING AHEAD

MEMORY VERSES: Matthew 11:28-30
BIBLE STUDY: Psalm 51
READING: Heartbreak

 Core Truth

What is the crucial starting point that enables us to grow in our love for God and our neighbor?

The Scriptures tell us that our immense Lord not only dwells in the highest heaven but is also magnetically drawn to the smallest heart (Isaiah 57:15). Our hearts roll out the welcome mat to God's indwelling presence when they are marked by a broken and contrite spirit. We who are broken-hearted are essentially grief-stricken over our capacity for sin (Jeremiah 17:9), and yet our contrite state makes us the object of the Lord's reviving mercy.

1. Identify key words or phrases in the question and answer above, and state their meaning in your own words.

2. Restate the core truth in your own words.

3. What questions or issues does the core truth raise for you?

📖 Memory Verse Study Guide

Jesus is the embodiment of humility. He lived in a state of constant communion with his Father and desired to do only his Father's will. The Father's pleasure in his Son, in turn, formed the foundation for Jesus' quality of life on earth. In our memory verses, Jesus invites us into that same life of "rest for our souls" that he experienced with his Father.

1. *Putting it in context:* Read Matthew 11:25-27. These verses provide the setting for our memory verses. How would you characterize Jesus' relationship with his Father?

2. The memory verses are *Matthew 11:28-30.* Copy the verses verbatim.

3. Jesus issues an invitation to the "weary and burdened." What state of heart do you think these words refer to?

4. Jesus offers "rest" to those who come to him. What kind of "rest" is he talking about?

5. What do you think Jesus means by "take my yoke upon you and learn from me"? What is Jesus' yoke? (Take a look at some commentaries to get the meaning of *yoke.*)

6. How does Jesus describe himself? How are these qualities able to provide rest?

7. What would it mean for you to respond to Jesus' invitation to "come to me"? Can you identify where you might be "weary and burdened" in your soul? Where do you need rest?

Inductive Bible Study Guide

King David serves as a helpful biblical model of one whose will is yielded to God. In Pisidian Antioch, Paul recounts the Old Testament story line which includes this testimony to David: "After removing Saul, he made David their king. He testified concerning him: 'I have found David son of Jesse a man after my own heart; he will do everything I want him to do'" (Acts 13:22). Yet David walked a very painful path to become the man whose heart was aligned with God's. For the backdrop to Psalm 51, read the story of David's betrayal of his core beliefs in 2 Samuel 11–12.

Psalm 51 is known as one of the penitential or confessional psalms. In it David pours out his heart with a stark honesty that leads him to cast himself on the mercy of God. He takes us on his journey of restoration and shows us the broken and contrite heart to which God is attracted and in which God desires to dwell.

1. *Read Psalm 51.* Recount the stark honesty with which David has come to terms with his sin.

   Of what need is he fully aware (vv. 1-5)?

2. To what qualities of God does David appeal as a basis for his restoration (vv. 1-2)?

3. In verses 7-12, what does David plead with God to do for him?

   In your own words, what do you sense David is longing for?

4. In verse 17 David identifies sacrifices that God "will not despise." What is the nature of the heart that is acceptable to God?

5. Capture in your own words or images how you would describe the heart that God desires.

6. Where in this psalm does David express your own needs and longings?

Reading: Heartbreak

What is the fundamental starting point when it comes to loving God with all our heart, soul, mind and strength and loving our neighbor as ourselves? In other words, what is *the* issue that, if not addressed at the very beginning of our journey together, will make this study meaningless?

I have positioned as our first consideration the need for a broken and contrite heart because without it, our love for God and others simply can't grow. It is as simple as that. Starkly put, *if you bypass this truth, you will be wasting your time.*

OUR BIG GOD DWELLS IN SMALL HEARTS

Scripture tells us that there is actually a heart condition to which God is attracted or drawn. In other words, there is a state of the heart which allows our Lord to most readily and comfortably take up residence within us: *a broken heart.* A theme that runs through the Old and into the New Testament is that our big God is drawn to the smallest of hearts, the one that recognizes its unworthiness.

Let's quickly trace this biblical theme and then land on it as exemplified in the person of King David. The first two references come from the prophet Isaiah.

This is what the LORD says:

> "Heaven is my throne,
>   and the earth is my footstool.
> Where is the house you will build for
>   me?

> Where will my resting place be?
> Has not my hand made all these
>   things,
>   and so they came into being?"
>   declares the LORD.

> "This is the one I esteem:
>   he who is humble and contrite in
>   spirit,
>   and trembles at my word." (Isaiah
>   66:1-2)

> For this is what the high and lofty
>   One says—
>   he who lives forever, whose name
>   is holy:
> "I live in a high and holy place,
>   but also with him who is contrite
>   and lowly in spirit,
> to revive the spirit of the lowly
>   and to revive the heart of the
>   contrite." (Isaiah 57:15)

When Jesus laid out the vision of life in the kingdom of God, he described those who would be comfortable in his kingdom through what are called the Beatitudes. What are the "attitudes of being" that are consistent with God's kingdom values? The very first Beatitude is, intentionally, "Blessed are the poor in spirit, for theirs is the kingdom of heaven" (Matthew 5:3). The word *blessed* does not have a ready equivalent in the English language, but some suggested synonyms are *happy, fortunate* or *congratulated.* The one I like the best, though, is Karl Barth's translation: "You lucky bums . . . are the poor in spirit, for the kingdom of God is opened to you."[1] Simply put, the way into the kingdom of God is on our knees. Those who realize their spiritual destitution, who come to God with empty hands and without human resources, are actually the ones who find great resonance within God's kingdom. Jesus did, after all, say of himself, "I am gentle and humble in heart" (Matthew 11:29). The brokenhearted find in the heart of Jesus a welcome presence.

KING DAVID'S TRAGEDY

The biblical character who perhaps best exemplifies a heart truly broken over sin and from whom we can learn the most in this area is King David. In Psalm 51:17 David, writing from personal experience, acknowledged, "The sacrifices of God are a broken spirit; a broken and contrite heart, O God, you will not despise."

How did David come to personally understand this truth? How was his heart broken? David wrote Psalm 32 and 51 against the backdrop of a tragic moral failure that brought him face to face with the darkness in his own spirit and led to his broken heart.

His story is recorded in excruciating detail in 2 Samuel 11 and 12. We are told first that it was spring, when the kings normally led their troops in battle against the neighboring nomadic tribes. Instead of going himself, however, David sent his army off under Joab, his commander. Having idle time, which is the devil's playground, David spied from his rooftop one evening a beautiful woman, Bathsheba, bathing. Overcome with passion, he abused the power of his office to have her brought to him and then forced himself on her, with full knowledge that she was another man's wife.

This misdeed led to an avalanche of treachery. He soon received a report back from Bathsheba that she was pregnant—and so the cover-up commenced. Attempting to hide the fact that he was the father of the child, David called Uriah, Bathsheba's husband, back from the frontlines of battle where he had been under Joab's command. He thought that if he could get Uriah to sleep with his wife, Uriah would be none the wiser, and the deception would be complete. But Uriah refused the pleasures of his home life after two attempts on David's part, saying, "The ark and Israel and Judah are staying in tents, and my master Joab and my lord's men are camped in the open fields. How could I go to my house to eat and drink and lie with my wife?" (2 Samuel 11:11). David must have been shamed by his servant's great loyalty.

David then shifted to plan B, only to dig a deeper hole. He sent Uriah back to Joab, placing in his hands sealed instructions that contained Uriah's own death warrant. Joab was ordered to place Uriah in the thick of the fiercest conflict. Then, when the battle reached its zenith, his fellow soldiers were to withdraw from him, leaving Uriah exposed, so that he'd be killed in battle.

Sir Walter Scott once wrote, "Oh! What a tangled web we weave, when first we practice to deceive." David certainly illustrates this principle. In a short period of time, David went from abusing his power to raping a woman, plotting murder and, all along the way, bringing in accessories to help him, even implicating them in his deeds at points. And this is the man of whom God said, "The LORD has sought out a man after his own heart and appointed him leader of his people" and "I have found David son of Jesse a man after my own heart; he will do everything I want him to do" (1 Samuel 13:14; Acts 13:22).

How could this possibly be? David's self-inflicted pain brought him to a place of having a "broken and contrite heart."

KING DAVID'S CONFESSION

David had a conscience that was finely tuned to God's heart, and we know from his own self-reflection that he couldn't live with what he had done. In Psalm 32 he tells of the psychological and spiritual trauma that he brought on himself for approximately a year following his horrendous acts. He essentially became a fugitive from God. As the Lord pressed in on him, David wrote, "When I kept silent, my bones wasted away through my groaning all day long. For day and night your hand was heavy upon me; my strength was sapped as in the heat of summer" (Psalm 32:3-4). Here was a man haunted by guilt, sapped of energy, because he was living with the discrepancy between what he knew was right and his degrading behavior. As someone once observed, "You can't go against the grain of the universe without getting splinters."

It was during that time that the Lord set a trap for David. The prophet Nathan had been informed by the Lord of what David had done, so he proceeded to tell him a story about a wealthy man and a very poor man. The rich man had many sheep and cattle, but the poor man only had one lone treasured possession, a little ewe lamb that had become a household pet, beloved by his children. An out-of-town guest came to see the rich man. Wanting to entertain him but not diminish his own resources, the rich man forcibly took the little lamb from the poor man and then had it slaughtered, dressed and prepared for his visitor.

David took the bait. He didn't see it coming. He seethed with righteous indignation over the dastardly deed of the rich man, asserting that he deserved to die. Then Nathan, pausing for just the right dramatic moment, said to David, "You are the man! . . . Why did you despise the word of the LORD by doing what is evil in his eyes? You struck down Uriah the Hittite with the sword and took his wife to be your own" (2 Samuel 12:7, 9).

There was no place for David to hide. He was caught red-handed. Exposed. There was no way out. Perhaps, then, it was with a sense of relief that David stated unequivocally, "I have sinned against the LORD" (2 Samuel 12:13). No excuses. No justification. In Psalm 32:5 he wrote, "I acknowledged my sin to you and did not cover up my iniquity. I said, 'I will confess my transgressions to the LORD.'"

In light of all this, how is it that David

can be called "a man after God's own heart"? Perhaps this was his defining moment, the moment when he came to terms with himself, when his heart was cracked open in a way that made him available to God like never before. Most often it is the hurts we bring upon ourselves that lead us to where we need to go.

CHARACTERISTICS OF A BROKEN AND CONTRITE HEART

I've identified four characteristics of a "broken and contrite heart"—the kind of heart in which God takes up residence and which he is attracted to.

1. A person with a broken heart has given up the pretense of pretended goodness. David finally had the privilege (and I choose this word carefully) of seeing the extent of the evil—evil that violated his most cherished principles—that he was capable of. He peered starkly into the abyss of his own heart. If Nathan the prophet had come to him ahead of time to warn him of the temptation that Bathsheba would present, my guess is that David would have protested loudly, "There's no way I'm going to intentionally violate the commandments that prohibit committing adultery, giving false testimony against my neighbor, coveting my neighbor's wife and committing murder. Won't happen! That is not me."

To have a broken heart is to be stripped of any false notions regarding our capacity for sin. Tending to judge ourselves on the basis of the bad deeds we have avoided, we may carry around a subtle pride that we would never do the kind of thing David did. *I have never committed adultery or murder,* we say to ourselves, *so I am a fairly decent person.* But what if we measured ourselves against the opportunities missed?

Traditionally, sin has been divided into the two categories of "sins of commission" and "sins of omission." It is the sins of omission that we fail to recognize and which may be an even greater indicator of what state our heart is in. What if we measured the state of our heart based on the extent of our hardness to what we could or should do? These are the sins of missed opportunities. We know, for example, that people are dying of hunger across this globe while we are well fed, but we're not necessarily moved to alleviate this condition. We can go merrily about our business, living in our comfort, knowing all along that there are kids born as orphans being raised by siblings who are kids themselves. Yet we sleep at night. To do so we have to close our hearts to these needs to a certain extent.

Perhaps one of the most difficult things to do is to make an accurate estimate of ourselves. Socrates famously said, "The unexamined life is not worth living." True, but self-examination is enormously tough and requires hard work. We tend to want to see ourselves in the best possible light. Let me illustrate from personal experience. In my high school and college years I played some competitive tennis. I would win some and lose some. Yet every tenth match or so, I would play out of my mind.

All the shots found their proper location. It would seem I couldn't miss. So who was the real tennis player? Of course it was the one who was at the height of invincibility. *That's the real me,* I told myself. In point of fact, I was a mediocre tennis player at best. But I so wanted to see myself through the lens of my rare invulnerability.

How hard it is for us to look at the state of our soul!

Yehiel Dinur's story serves as a window into every person's heart. Dinur was a witness at the trial of Adolf Eichmann, a butcher of the Jews during World War II. The courtroom was hushed when Dinur entered and stared at the man behind the bullet-proof glass. Then dramatically and suddenly, Dinur began to sob, and collapsed to the floor. Everyone assumed that Dinur was reliving the horrors of the gas chambers, but he later explained that that wasn't it at all. "I was afraid about myself," he said. "I saw that I am capable to do this . . . exactly like he." Then with chilling clarity Dinur added, "Eichmann is in all of us."[2]

Most of us are not usually willing to be as honest about our hearts as Dinur was. It takes work to get to a place of such honesty. Those who have experienced the redemption of a twelve-step program know just how much work is required; they tell us that it's pretty difficult just to get to step one, which is confessing that we are powerless over _____ (fill in the blank). Then, the painful fifth step requires a no-holds-barred confession to another person in the program, due to the program's belief that "you are as sick as your sickest secret and you remain sick as long as it remains a secret." We *need* confession, to be sure—but oh, the humility and humiliation of it all, to finally acknowledge that you can't defeat what is destroying you.

When we're finally willing to confess our sin, however, we can find freedom. David was clearly free when he could write, "For I know my transgressions, and my sin is always before me. Against you, you only, have I sinned and done what is evil in your sight, so that you are proved right when you speak and justified when you judge. Surely I was sinful at birth, sinful from the time my mother conceived me" (Psalm 51:3-5).

This raw honesty seems to be the key to opening up the storehouse of God's mercy. *Blessed is the one who has lost the façade of pretended goodness.*

2. The person with a "broken and contrite heart" has no room for self-righteous judgment of others. Jesus told the story of the elder brother in the parable of the prodigal son to show the Pharisees their self-righteous hearts of haughty condemnation. The Pharisees had established themselves as the standard bearers of righteousness, the protectors of the law, and from this lofty perch they looked down upon all those who were not as diligent as they were. But when you have come to terms with your own heart, there is no room for judgment.

No one has defined more clearly or succinctly the distinction between the proud and humble heart than Jonathan Edwards, the great Puritan preacher of the First Great Awakening. He says it so well that it simply stands on its own:

> Spiritual pride is very apt to suspect others; whereas an humble saint is most jealous of himself, he is so suspicious of nothing in the world as he is of his own heart. The spiritually proud person is apt to find fault with other saints, that they are low in grace; and to be much in observing how cold and dead they are; and being quick to discern and take notice of their deficiencies. But the eminently humble Christian has so much to do at home . . . that he is not apt to be very busy with other hearts.[3]

When we come face to face with ourselves, we know that we have a lifetime of work to do within and therefore don't have time to look down on others. We are in a position to help others out of their weaknesses, but we're not in a position to bruise others with our judgment or condemnation.

And so we simply say with David, who, like us, had no moral high ground from which to condemn others, "Have mercy on *me,* O God, according to your unfailing love; according to your great compassion blot out *my* transgressions. Wash away all *my* iniquity and cleanse *me* from *my* sin" (Psalm 51:1-2).

This leads us to the third characteristic of a humble heart.

3. Those whose hearts have been broken are eminently teachable. David's heart was made pliable and moldable. The heart of stone was replaced with a heart of flesh. He writes in Psalm 51:6, "Surely you desire truth in the inner parts; you teach me wisdom in the inmost place."

Are our hearts eager to live in truth? Have you ever had someone say to you in response to an inquiry you made of them, "Well, do you want the truth, or should I lie and make you feel good?" Doesn't every part of your body inwardly scream, "Lie and make me feel good!"? But then, upon further reflection, we brace ourselves and say, "No, I better hear the truth."

Do we seek the truth, invite the truth . . . about ourselves? In recent months I've sometimes wondered how I come across to people. What is the impact of my personality on others around me? If I were to describe myself to others would my description match how others think of me? I'm not sure. So let me offer this challenge to you: If you want to be a friend of truth, go to the people whom you trust, who have your best interest at heart, and ask them, "If you knew I wouldn't get defensive and angry, what hard truth would you like to tell me? Is there something you've been wanting to say to me but haven't dared to because of how you thought I might react? Well, now's your chance." Do we want truth that much?

4. Finally, the humble and contrite heart draws the delight of the Father. This is the true irony of the gospel. God never seems to be more pleased with us than when we acknowledge that our greatest need is for him.

David wrote Psalms 32 and 51 as a liberated person experiencing the renewed pleasure and delight of the Father's welcome and forgiveness. Psalm 32, for example, starts with, "Blessed is he whose transgressions are forgiven, whose sins are covered. Blessed is the man whose sin the LORD does not count against him and in whose spirit is no deceit" (vv. 1-2). Then in Psalm 51 David writes, "Let me hear joy and gladness; let the bones you have crushed rejoice. . . . Restore to me the joy of your salvation" (vv. 8, 12).

In David's dialogue with Nathan, as soon as David said "I have sinned against the LORD," what were the next words out of Nathan's mouth? "And you will burn in hell because of it." No, a thousand times no! Nathan speaks on behalf of God, reassuring David, "The LORD has taken away your sin" (2 Samuel 12:13). Of course, there were consequences, but God was no longer an enemy to run from; he was a Father whose arms David could run to.

It is a wondrous thing that unvarnished repentance leads to the open-hearted welcome. Max Lucado illustrates this well through a story that originates in Brazil. Maria had raised her daughter Christina since Christina was a baby in the aftermath of her husband's death. Scratching out a living as a maid, Maria provided a loving home for her daughter. But Christina was an independent spirit. She couldn't imagine marrying a young man from her rural village and settling down to raise a family there. The big city beckoned; she dreamed of the bright lights and the excitement of Rio.

Maria had warned Christina about what waited for her there. Jobs were scarce. How would she support herself? She knew what Christina would have to resort to if she went to the city. Her heart therefore sank when she awoke one morning to discover that Christina was gone. Immediately she knew that she would have to go looking for her daughter, so she gathered up a few belongings, took all the money she had and scampered out the door. As she was leaving town she stopped by a cheap photo booth to take some pictures of herself.

Knowing that her daughter was too proud to give up, Maria began to search for Christina in bars, hotels, nightclubs—all the places where prostitutes hang out. And she left her picture everywhere she went: on a bathroom mirror, on a hotel bulletin board, in a phone booth. On the back of each picture she wrote a note. When Maria's money ran out and no daughter was found, she returned home.

A few weeks later, a tired Christina walked down a flight of hotel stairs. Her eyes spoke of pain and fear, as her dream had become a nightmare. When she reached the bottom of the stairs, she spotted a familiar face. On the lobby mirror was a small black-and-white photo of her mother. Removing the picture, she turned it over to read these words: "Whatever you have done, whatever you have become, it doesn't matter. Please come home."[4]

God is never more pleased with us than when we acknowledge our need of him.

The broken and contrite heart is the heart to which God is drawn, and in which God dwells most richly, because it is a heart that recognizes our sinful capacity, has given up the moral high ground of judgment, is seeking to live in the truth and lives in the joy of the Father's delight.

---

[1]Quoted by Darrell Johnson in a sermon on the Sermon on the Mount.

[2]"The Enduring Revolution," Templeton Address delivered by Charles W. Colson at the University of Chicago, September 2, 1993.

[3]Quoted in Richard Lovelace, *Dynamics of Spiritual Life: An Evangelical Theology of Renewal* (Downers Grove, Ill.: InterVarsity Press, 1979), pp. 245-46.

[4]Max Lucado, *No Wonder They Call Him Savior* (Portland, Ore.: Multnomah, 1986), p. 157.

Reading Study Guide

1. Why is the broken and contrite heart the most important starting point on the way to a deeper love for God and our neighbor?

2. In light of David's tragic moral failure, how could he be called "a man after God's own heart"?

3. This reading identified four characteristics of a heart that is broken and contrite. Put your understanding of each of them in your own words:

   • Loss of pretended goodness:

   • Absence of self-righteous judgment:

   • Eminently teachable:

   • God's delight in us:

4. As you look at this list, where do you observe these characteristics in your life?

5. Where do you see that the Lord has more work to do in you to get you to the place where you are wide open to his work in your life?

3 / A Listening Heart

LOOKING AHEAD

MEMORY VERSES: John 15:9-11
BIBLE STUDY: Luke 10:38-42; John 10:1-18
READING: The Heart That Listens

 Core Truth

How do disciples align their hearts with the heart of God?

The goal of a disciple is to grow to the point where the will of God is simply a reflexive, automatic response in the midst of life's daily circumstances. We learn to respond from a deep godly center indirectly by practicing the spiritual disciplines that address the inner regions of our decision-making center. Ultimately these practices put us in the position to listen to the voice of Jesus.

1. Identify key words or phrases in the question and answer above, and state their meaning in your own words.

2. Restate the core truth in your own words.

3. What questions or issues does the core truth raise for you?

Memory Verse Study Guide

In John 15, our Lord uses the image of the vine and the branches as a way to teach about the necessity of staying connected to him as the life source. The goal of the Christian life, Jesus tells us, is to "bear much fruit" (John 15:8). This fruit is both quantitative (more disciples) and qualitative (better disciples). The evidence that we are bearing much fruit is love for God, demonstrated through obedience to his will.

1. *Putting it in context:* After reading John 15:1-8, put in your own words your understanding of the relationship between Jesus (the vine) and us (the branches).

2. The memory verses are *John 15:9-11*. Copy the verses verbatim.

3. Jesus tells us that we are to remain in his love in the same way that he has remained in the Father's love. How do we do that?

4. What is the relationship between obedience and love?

5. In verse 11 Jesus says that the benefit of obedience is to have his joy in us. What was the joy of Jesus (see John 4:31-34; 15:9; Hebrews 12:1-4)?

6. Based upon our understanding of what Jesus' joy is, how does our joy become "complete"?

7. What do these verses teach us about the way we go about aligning our hearts with the heart of Jesus?

Inductive Bible Study Guide

Our Bible study focuses on two Scripture texts about the listening, attentive heart. First we'll look at a passage on Mary and Martha, chosen because of the indelible contrasting image it provides. Mary sits at the feet of Jesus while Martha scurries around nervously attending to household duties. In our society, the practice of silence and solitude gets drowned out by the frenetic activity that marks most of our lives. In our second text from John 10, Jesus tells us that we can actually learn to hear and follow the tone of his voice in contrast to the voices of others who beckon us to follow them.

1. *Read Luke 10:38-42*. Describe the contrasting behavior of Mary and Martha when Jesus came to visit their home.

2. How does Martha embody the nature of life today? What is Jesus' diagnosis for what is going on in Martha's spirit?

3. Mary is commended for the role she has chosen. Put in your own words the state of Mary's heart. What is the lesson here for us?

4. *Read John 10:1-18*. Describe the relationship the sheep have with the true shepherd.

5. Throughout this passage Jesus contrasts himself with a "stranger," a "thief" and a "hired hand." What are the characteristics of false shepherds?

6. What are the distinguishing characteristics of the good shepherd?

7. Given the contrast between the false shepherds and the good shepherd, how would we know when the true shepherd is speaking to us? What does his voice sound like?

⬥ Reading: The Heart That Listens

A Native American was being escorted around the center of Manhattan in New York by a friend who was a resident of the city. The Native American stopped his friend and whispered, "Wait. I hear a cricket." His doubting friend said, "Come on. A cricket? With all the noise of the taxis, horns honking, brakes screeching and people screaming, you couldn't possibly hear a cricket." Undaunted, the Native American led his friend to a nearby planter and dug through the mulch, and sure enough, there was the cricket.

His friend said, "How could you possibly hear a cricket in downtown New York?" The Native American replied, "My ears are different than yours. It simply depends on what you are trained to listen to. Here, let me show you." With that he pulled a handful of change out of his pocket and dropped the coins on the sidewalk. When the coins clanked on the cement, everyone within a block turned around.

The obvious question is, What have our ears been trained to hear?

In the parable of the sower, Jesus teaches us about the significance of listening and allowing the word of God to take root in our life in depth (Mark 4:1-9, 13-20). He bookends the parable with the exhortation to listen: In verse 3, his introductory word is "Listen!" and in verse 9 he closes the first telling of the parable with, "He who has ears to hear, let him hear." Then, when Jesus interprets the meaning of the different kinds of soil, he connects each one to hearing the word. Four soils, four uses of the word *hear*. In other words, this parable is about the three kinds of soil that represent disruptions to our hearing of the word and a fourth kind of good soil that yields growth thirty-, sixty- and a hundredfold.

Before we get to the good soil that produces a listening heart, Jesus says that there are three ways that our ears get plugged. Our ears, he's saying, are the soil of our souls (to mix metaphors!). So we must ask ourselves, to what are our ears attuned?

THE HURRIED HEART

> The farmer sows the word. Some people are like seed along the path, where the word is sown. As soon as *they hear it,* Satan comes and takes away the word that was sown in them. (Mark 4:14-15).

In the agricultural land of Palestine, the fields were cut in serpentine (snake-like) strips divided by thin walkways which had been beaten down by human and animal feet. Baked under the sun, these pathways became hard as asphalt. As the sower casts the seed in his arclike motion, some of it falls on this impenetrable soil and simply bounces off. It is then easy prey for the birds, with which Jesus likens Satan.

This path represents the hardened heart, which can come about for many reasons but especially because of a hurried life. Paths were beaten down because they were well used. Frenetic feet marked these routes. The word of God can only penetrate to the extent that we stop, spend time in quiet solitude and contemplate its meaning. Richard Foster introduces his devotional classic *Celebration of Discipline* by putting his finger on a major issue in the Western world: "In contemporary society our Adversary majors in three things: noise, hurry, and crowds. If he can keep us engaged in 'muchness and manyness,' he will rest satisfied."[1] Do you ever wonder how people from other cultures view our way of life? What is normal for us seems odd to them. In fact, *mazungu,* the Swahili word for "white man," literally means "one who spins around."[2] East Africans see us as people in a flurry of motion going nowhere.

If hearing requires some time for quiet listening to God's word, ask yourself: Do I intentionally stop my feverish activity for a block of time each day to simply listen in stillness to God's Spirit or his word? Do you have a hurried heart?

THE SHALLOW HEART

Others, like seed sown on rocky places, *hear the word* and at once receive it with joy. But since they have no root, they last only a short time. When trouble or persecution comes because of the word, they quickly fall away. (Mark 4:16-17)

Israel is a land of rocks. There is a legend that the angel in charge of stone could not manage the weight and so dumped nine-tenths of his load on Israel. In much of southern Israel, a veneer of dirt covers the limestone that's just beneath the surface. The morning dew is enough to germinate the seed in the shallow soil, so a flower will spring to life, looking robust, until the heat of the day causes it to wither. Why? There is no place for the root to go when it hits the limestone floor.

Jesus is most likely speaking of those who enter the freshness of God's saving and renewing grace. At the beginning there is a warm glow of heart, a sense of being God's beloved child living under the spotlight of his glory. But then comes the discovery that this is only the beginning; the process of transformation is hard work. We want the benefits, but not the demands. We want a Christian faith without a cross.

To sink our roots into the soil of God's word requires us to take a look at those things that need to be changed in our lives, to face up to the hard work of confronting the darkness. As James Baldwin wrote, "Not everything can be changed, but nothing can be changed until it is faced."[3] The biblical word for change or growth is *repentance,* which literally means to have a change of mind, to think differently, to have a second thought that corrects a first thought.

The one with the shallow heart wants simply to look good without having to be good. We want what God can do for us but not God himself. Does this describe you and me? To use a football illustration, do we want a God who is our blocking back, knocking down all potential opposing tacklers so that we can run for touchdowns and raise our arms in continuous celebration? Then we have miscalculated the Christian life. There is not enough root to sustain us.

THE DIVIDED HEART

> Still others, like seed sown among thorns, *hear the word;* but the worries of this life, the deceitfulness of wealth and the desires for other things come in and choke the word, making it unfruitful. (Mark 4:18-19)

In Jesus' day, farmers had a practice of cutting off the tops of fibrous rooted weeds and then burning the remains so that the ground looked clean. Seeds that landed in this area would sprout, but then seasonal rains would cause rapid growth of the unseen thorny weeds, choking the life out of the wheat crop.

Now Jesus starts to meddle in our way of life. Is there anything that can plug up our ears more than the distraction of worry or the pursuit of things?

Fear or worry creates static on the line of our connection with God. Don't we experience anxiety as static in the stomach? In my journey toward Christlike wholeness, there has been no greater enemy than a diffuse anxiety that resided in my gut. This anxiety cut me off from the experiential reality that I am a beloved child of God and caused me to experience this world as a fearful, dangerous and unsafe place. I finally had to seek help from trusted Christian friends and colleagues and ask them to pray that I would know the healing reality that I live under the pleasure of the Father's delight.

Unless this issue of anxiety is addressed, we will be distracted by debilitating pictures of a worrisome future. We need to hear the same message that the Father delivered to his Son at the inauguration of his ministry as he came out of the waters of John's baptism: "You are my Son, chosen and marked by my love, pride of my life" (Mark 1:11 *The Message*). Until we can be embraced by this message, many of us will be distracted by "the worries of this life."

Jesus then speaks to "the deceitfulness of wealth and the desire for other things," which is essentially a description of Western affluence today. A short story illustrates this Western mindset well: A young man proposed to the woman who had stolen his heart. "Darling," he said. "I want you to know that I love you more than anything else in all the world. I want you to marry me. I am not rich. I don't have a yacht or Rolls-Royce like Johnny Brown, but I do love you with all my heart." The young woman thought for a moment and replied, "I love you too, but tell me more about Johnny Brown."

This is the fault line for many of us. This is the place where the battle is being waged in our heart. Is our longing for and pursuit of comfort and things what chokes the life out of the hearing of God's word? A great preacher in the early part of the last century, Harry Emerson Fosdick, spoke to this, saying something to the effect of, "As long as what the world has to offer has more glitter than the promise of Christian life, then Christianity doesn't have a chance."

Is there a battle still waging over our souls? Are we caught in the taffy pull of the allure of this world and the desire to be Christ's person? Frankly, we may never put this battle to rest, but who is winning? Which has the greater draw—what the world has to offer or what Jesus promises to do in us?

THE LISTENING HEART

In contrast to these three states of heart that disrupt the hearing of the word, the fruitful heart is the listening heart. Mark 4:20 says, "Others, like seed sown on good soil, *hear the word,* accept it, and produce a crop—thirty, sixty or even a hundred times what was sown." The good soil is where the plow has cut a deep furrow into the ground and turned over the soil, so that the seed can sink deeply in and take root.

What makes for good soil—for growth that's continuous and intentional? How do we develop a listening heart? First, we must become *self-aware.* Listening and self-awareness are integrally related. The apostle Paul put it like this: "I say to every one of you: Do not think of yourself more highly than you ought, but rather

think of yourself with sober judgment" (Romans 12:3). In other words, remain in reality, not in a fantasy land about yourself. We can allow the Holy Spirit's searchlight to examine our hearts fully; we will never discern anything about ourselves that God does not already know—and yet he has decided to love us anyway (Romans 5:8). This allows us to remain in the truth about who we are and where we need to grow.

John Calvin, one of the fathers of the Reformation, wrote a classic tome titled *Institutes of the Christian Religion.* His very first caption is, "Without knowledge of self, there is no knowledge of God." He goes on to say in the first line that follows, "Nearly all the wisdom we possess . . . consists of two parts: the knowledge of God and the knowledge of self."[4] They are interactive: knowledge of self leads to knowledge of God and vice versa.

If knowledge of God and self is necessary to develop a listening heart, the question that naturally follows is, How do we develop this deeper knowledge of God and ourselves? The answer, simply put, is spiritual disciplines. I would compare spiritual disciplines to listening posts: ways or practices that we can build into our life to help us hear what God is saying to us. Let me propose four listening posts—means of attuning ourselves to God's wavelengths or signals—to assist our intentional growth toward deep hearing.

Listening post 1: Place your life up next to the truth of Scripture. Every day read some portion of the Scripture with the attitude, "Lord, show me the truth about myself from your Word." Paul tells us the purpose of Scripture in 2 Timothy 3:16-17: "All Scripture is God-breathed and is useful for teaching, rebuking, correcting and training in righteousness, so that all God's people may be thoroughly equipped for every good work" (TNIV).

Note the second and third characteristics of Scripture. The Scripture *reproves* and *corrects*. What is reproof? It is a rebuke. Gordon MacDonald, in his book *Restoring Your Spiritual Passion,* says that "one good rebuke is worth a 100 affirmations."[5] Have you ever been reading the Bible and, all of a sudden, felt as if there was a figurative knife in your heart because the truth so clearly revealed some shortcoming you knew you needed to pay attention to? This is why James compares the Scripture to looking in a mirror: "Don't fool yourself into thinking that you are a listener when you are anything but, letting the Word go in one ear and out the other. Act on what you hear! Those who hear and don't act are like those who glance in the mirror, walk away, and two minutes later have no idea who they are, what they look like" (James 1:22-24 *The Message*). When we read the Scriptures we are holding a mirror up to our faces. We must refuse to turn away and forget what we look like.

The good news is that this mirror into which we look also shows the image of Jesus standing behind us, the One who desires to reflect his image through us. So pick up a devotional book, adopt a reading plan—in some way, make room to listen to God's Word for you.

Listening post 2: Develop the discipline of silence and solitude in order to listen deeply. The psalmist says, "For God alone my soul waits in silence" (Psalm 62:1 ESV). And Henri Nouwen has written, "Without solitude it is virtually impossible to live a spiritual life."[6] If we are not used to silence—and most of us aren't—this will be some of the hardest work that we do. Our first attempts at being quiet before God will surface a lot of static and noise, because we are so used to filling our lives with input.

Like in the movie *What About Bob?* we may need "baby steps" here. One of the breakthroughs I have had in solitude and silence has come from adopting the practice of the prayer of examen, or the examination of consciousness. The idea here is to either conclude your day or begin the next day (which is what I do) by pausing to look back through a God-directed tour of the previous day's events, relationships and emotions. In Adele Calhoun's book *Spiritual Disciplines Handbook* she says that "the examen provides a way of noticing where God shows up in our day. It is a practice that attends to what we might otherwise miss in the press of duties and busyness."[7]

Have you ever been asked how your week was and been unable to answer because your consciousness felt like one big blur, and nothing immediately stood out? Time passes, but what in that time is worth paying attention to? We turn page after page of our lives, but we have not been sensitive to where God has been in them. The prayer of examen tells us to slow down. Before you turn the page on a new day, pause to reread yesterday's page. I call this "praying backwards." In my journal, I simply ask the Lord, What do you want me to pay attention to? Where were you present in this day? I often find that the Lord brings to mind things and people for which I should be thankful. In addition, I might have missed an opportunity to share a word of grace and encouragement. I follow up with a note of gratitude.

Here are a few of the questions that Adele Calhoun suggests we ask the Lord:

1. For what moment today am I most grateful? For what moment today am I least grateful?

2. When did I give and receive love today? When did I fail to give and receive love?

3. What was the most life-giving or life-thwarting part of my day?

The practice of examen is a great way to bring our lives before God in silence and have him to speak us.

Listening post 3: Intertwine your life with trusted Christian friends who will help you live in truth. Henry Cloud and John Townsend address the place that trusted Christian friends have in helping us listen to God's voice in their book *How People Grow*. In the chapter titled "God's Plan A: People," Henry writes autobiographically about how he began his Christian walk in a state of depression. He confessed to a friend that he had asked God to help him, but he wasn't feeling any better and, quite frankly, felt like God had let him down. His friend suggested a married couple who might be of help.

This couple invested in Henry. He says of them, "Bill taught me about God, and Julie taught me about life." As he opened up to them, he got in touch with a deep sadness and grief over a lost dream. They allowed him to explore feelings that he didn't even know he had. As a result of their encouragement, he got involved in a small group and began to examine himself through the feedback he was receiving about how he came across. His self-awareness increased through the reflections from others whose heart intentions he trusted.

One day Henry realized that his depression had lifted and the feeling of emptiness had vanished. "I actually felt good about life and about me," he writes. But he still held God accountable for not healing him directly. Then he realized that God's Plan A was people:

> I was waiting for God to give me his grace through supernatural zapping; he was giving it to me through his people. I was waiting for him to speak to me directly; he was speaking to me through his people. I was waiting for him to give me direction in life; He was the strength behind the direction people were giving me. I was waiting for him to heal my depres-

sion; he sent special people to comfort me.[8]

The church is built upon the belief that to live out our growth in Christ we must have a small group of trusted fellow Christian lovers who will speak into our life as needed.

Listening post 4: We will need to take faith risks by putting ourselves in uncomfortable places. As long as we remain in the safe confines of what's comfortable, minimal growth and self-awareness will occur. Many of us look at faith like a friend of mine did. He said, "I see faith like a spare tire. It is nice to have it there if I need it, but I sure hope I never have to use it." Faith for him was the safety net: God will catch me if the bottom falls out. The rest of the time he could be in charge of his own life, and stay within the predictable.

Biblical faith, however, compels us to take risks. To move out. To go to territory we have not been to before. In the faith chapter of Hebrews 11 we read that "by faith Abraham, when called to go to a place he would later receive as his inheritance, obeyed and went, even though he did not know where he was going" (v. 8). Biblical faith moves us by God's Spirit to obey, perhaps by going on a mission trip into the inner city or to another culture that will require us to exercise gifts and trust in him. Or biblical faith may require us to speak up for our faith in the context of the workplace, or stand by our values when we are asked to compromise.

If God seems distant and dull, it is probably because we have become distant and dull by remaining in a cocoon of safety. God meets us on the stretch.

Conclusion

There is only one condition of growth: *deep listening to the Word and obeying it.* Jesus tells us that there are three ways we tune God out: a hurried heart (being too busy to listen), a shallow heart (wanting benefits from God without demands) and a divided heart (being distracted by worry and the lure of the world).

If we want to listen we need to create listening posts:

1. Spend time looking into the mirror of God's Word.

2. Find quiet spaces to reflect on how God is at work daily.

3. Root our lives in trusting community with others who will speak truth to us.

4. Step out to explore territory into which God is calling us.

Growth in Christ is an intentional process that is usually incremental and uneven. This is why I like the story of the medieval peasant woman who happened to meet a Benedictine monk. She fell down before the monk and blurted out, "Please tell me, holy father, what do you men of God do up there in the monastery on the hill?" This particular monk was wise and humble, so he answered simply, "I'll tell you, my child, what we do: We fall down and we get up! We fall down and we get up!

We fall down and we get up!" Isn't that the way we grow?

Martin Luther King Jr. often concluded his talks with an old slave's prayer that gives us helpful perspective for the journey: "O God, I ain't what I ought to be and I ain't what I am gonna be; but thanks be to you, I ain't what I used to be!"

---

[1]Richard Foster, *Celebration of Discipline: The Path to Spiritual Growth* (San Francisco: Harper & Row, 1978), p. 13.

[2]Mark Buchanan, *The Rest of God: Restoring Your Soul by Restoring Sabbath* (Nashville: Thomas Nelson, 2006), p. 196.

[3]James Baldwin, quoted in Tim Hansel, *Dancin' Toward the Dawn: Discovering Joy in the Darkness of Loneliness* (Wheaton, Ill.: Victor, 2000), p. 105.

[4]John Calvin, *Institutes of the Christian Religion* 1.35.

[5]Gordon MacDonald, *Restoring Your Spiritual Passion* (Nashville: Thomas Nelson, 1986), p. 191.

[6]Henri Nouwen, quoted in Ruth Haley Barton, *Invitation to Solitude and Silence* (Downers Grove, Ill.: InterVarsity Press, 2004), p. 34.

[7]Adele Ahlberg Calhoun, *Spiritual Disciplines Handbook: Practices That Transform Us* (Downers Grove, Ill.: InterVarsity Press, 2005), p. 53.

[8]Henry Cloud and John Townsend, *How People Grow* (Grand Rapids: Zondervan, 2001), p. 120.

Reading Study Guide

1. Why do you suppose listening is so integral to obedience?

2. The reading discusses three ways that the hearing of the word is thwarted. What disruption to our hearing does each of these represent?

   a. The hurried heart (Mark 4:14-15)

   b. The shallow heart (Mark 4:16-17)

   c. The divided heart (Mark 4:18-19)

3. Where did you see yourself in these challenges that keep us from listening well to God's voice?

4. The reading asserts that self-awareness and listening are inseparable. What is the relationship between self-awareness and listening? Why might self-awareness be a key to continuous growth?

5. Look at the four listening posts that are suggested to keep us connected to the truth. Which one of these do you think holds the most promise for you? How can you incorporate that spiritual practice into your life?

Going Deeper

Calhoun, Adele Ahlberg. *Spiritual Disciplines Handbook: Practices That Transform Us.* Downers Grove, Ill.: InterVarsity Press, 2005. This book provides a comprehensive and practical guide to the historic practices that keep us tethered to God. Reverend Calhoun covers a wide array of categories including worship, opening up to God and sharing our life with others. This resource can serve as a "menu" for personal growth, or as a tool for practicing spiritual disciplines with others.

Part Two

LOVE THE LORD YOUR GOD . . .
WITH ALL YOUR SOUL

What is the soul? Jesus tells us to love God with all of our soul, but what does that mean? There are few concepts as elusive as the soul. Trying to understand it is like trying to hug a hologram; our arms go right through this image that seems to have no content. The heart, the mind and strength are more concrete because we can readily associate them with physical body parts. But where is the soul? With what do you associate it?

Our common understanding of the soul has been more influenced by Greek philosophy than Christian theology. Christian theology views our eternal destiny through the lens of the resurrection of the body. As we will discover in these next two chapters, this means that the soul encompasses and includes the body, as well as the heart and mind. The soul integrates the decision-making capacity of the heart, the lens through which we view life (the mind) and the energy of the body.

The Scripture doesn't teach that we *have* a soul; it teaches that we *are* souls, that we are "soulful" beings. At the very beginning in Genesis 2:7, God formed man from the earth and breathed into him a life-giving spirit. In other words, we are soulful creatures made up of heart, mind and body.

To make this more concrete, we will explore loving God with all of our soul in two major ways. We'll start with the common understanding of the soul as the depths of our being. If we want to express that something is coming from the core of our motivation, the very foundation of what is within us, it is our soul that we reference, as many of the psalms illustrate. For example, "Praise the LORD, O my soul; all my inmost being, praise his holy name" (Psalm 103). And "Why are you downcast, O my soul? Why so disturbed within me?" (Psalm 42).

With this idea of the soul as the very deepest part of us, we'll look at how our soul is ultimately only satisfied by the One who made us. We find our true satisfaction in communion and union with the One who has placed his image in us. In our first chapter on the soul, then, we will explore our *desire* for and *pursuit* of the God who alone can fulfill us.

The word *soul* is also used to simply describe us as persons, or to mean, essentially, "our life." We are soulful beings who have an identity and personhood. Thus, the words *life* and *soul* are interchangeable: "He who would save his life [soul] will lose it, and he who loses his life [soul] for my sake shall find it" (Luke 9:24). Jesus teaches us that we as persons only become the souls we were intended to be when we connect with the life *(zoe)* of God. Our souls come alive when injected with eternal life *(zoe)* found in relationship with Jesus Christ (John 17:3). In other words, only as the light of Christ shines through us can we become the unique souls, personalities, characters in God's play with all the color he intends. In the second chapter on the soul, then, we are going to explore how we become the *personalities* which God has prepared for us.

4 / A Soul That Thirsts for God

LOOKING AHEAD

MEMORY VERSES: Psalm 42:1-2
BIBLE STUDY: Isaiah 55
READING: Praise the Lord, O My Soul

 ## Core Truth

What does our soul long for most deeply?

Our soul's most basic craving is to be known and embraced by the God who made us for himself. The Bible captures this longing with the image of our souls as parched lands that thirst for the refreshing water that only the Lord himself can supply. To love God with all our soul is to acknowledge that he is the only ultimate satisfaction for our soul.

1. Identify key words or phrases in the question and answer above, and state their meaning in your own words.

2. Restate the core truth in your own words.

3. What questions or issues does the core truth raise for you?

Memory Verse Study Guide

Our memory verses are part of a psalm couplet tied together by a repeated refrain, "Why are you downcast, O my soul? Why so disturbed within me? Put your hope in God" (Psalm 42:5, 11; 43:5). The psalmist is evidently distressed and, you could say, even depressed. Yet he is crying out for the only One who can deliver him from his circumstances and bring ultimate satisfaction to his soul.

1. *Putting it in context:* Read Psalms 42 and 43. How would you describe the state of the psalmist's soul, and to what is he looking to pull himself out of this state?

2. The memory verses are *Psalm 42:1-2*. Copy the verses verbatim.

3. What words express the depth of the psalmist's desire?

4. How does the image of "thirst" capture this longing?

5. What does the psalmist seem to be missing?

6. Do you think thirst for God is a universal human experience? Why or why not?

7. Where in your life right now do you identify with the psalmist's longing?

✦ Inductive Bible Study Guide

The Lord, through the prophet Isaiah, issues a plaintive cry. Isaiah 55 simultaneously captures the longing of the heart for what will ultimately satisfy and recognizes that we are constantly settling for what can never deliver on its promise. Listen deeply not only to the longings of your soul, but also to the mournful pleading from God for us to receive the life he gives—the only life that leads to fullness and joy.

1. *Read Isaiah 55.* What is it that the Lord does not want us to miss out on?

2. What descriptive phrases capture the character of God throughout this passage?

3. What does the Lord promise to those who are "thirsty" and to those who "seek the Lord"?

4. How do you see people spending "money on what is not bread" and "labor on what does not satisfy"?

5. How do we miss what God wants for us?

6. The Lord promises that the richest of fare, wine and milk, can be purchased "without money and without cost." What is your understanding of what is being offered here?

7. What does this tell us about what it would require of us to receive the life-giving promises so graciously presented in this passage?

👓 Reading: Praise the Lord, O My Soul

From the wellspring of our *soul* flows our deepest desires.[1] To love God with all of our soul is to be captivated by the God who deserves our core affection. King David clearly makes this association in one of his psalms of praise when he says, "Praise the LORD, O my soul; *all my inmost being, praise his holy name*" (Psalm 103:1). Planted in the recesses of the human spirit is a longing to know and give highest honor to the One who has placed his stamp upon us. The writer of Ecclesiastes says that God "has also set eternity in the hearts of men" (Ecclesiastes 3:11). We bear the mark of the One who created us for himself, and we will never be satisfied until our souls are rooted in his life; there is a craving that must find fulfillment.

As I write these words the hour is approaching 1 p.m., and I am beginning to be distracted by an inner message that says, "Pay attention to these hunger pangs!" Even though I live comfortably and can satisfy my appetite on a whim, I know what hunger feels like and notice when my stomach is crying out for food. I must stop and pay attention to its incessant demand.

This gnawing hankering of hunger and thirst—a physical yearning common to all of us—is the dominant biblical image for our longing for God that emerges from both the Old and New Testament. A pair of psalms (which are now memorable worship choruses[2]) capture this basic ache of the soul: "As the deer pants for streams of water, so my soul *pants* for you, O God. My soul *thirsts* for God, for the living God. . . . O God, you are my God, earnestly I *seek* you; my soul *thirsts* for you, my body *longs* for you, in a dry and weary land where there is no water" (Psalm 42:1-2; 63:1). Then in the New Testament, Jesus tells us in the Beatitudes, "Blessed are those who *hunger* and *thirst* for righteousness, for they will be filled" (Matthew 5:6). In other words, Jesus is saying, "Blessed are those who hunger and thirst for me; to them I promise the reward of satisfaction." Similarly, in Jesus' encounter with the woman at the well, he entices her with an offering that awakens a longing she may not have even been conscious of: "Whoever drinks the water I give him will never *thirst*. Indeed, the water I give him will become in him a spring of water welling up to eternal life" (John 4:14). Later in John's Gospel, Jesus identifies this "water welling up to eternal life" with the promised gift of the Holy Spirit, and extends an invitation to every person on earth: "'If anyone is *thirsty*, let him come to me and drink. Whoever believes in me, as the Scripture has said, streams of living water will flow from within him'. By this he meant the Spirit" (John 7:37-39).

To love God with all of your soul is to seek to know more and more the One who alone can bring about satisfaction. This means that life is a journey that actually has a destination: being in relationship with our Creator and Redeemer. This fact is contrary to our cultural narrative that imagines life more like a bee simply flitting from flower to flower sucking in the nectar. Or as one Christian campus worker captured the cultural narrative, "It is fine to search for truth as long as you don't find it."

Yet this journey we call life does have a terminus, a purpose. There is a pearl of great price that is worth cashing in all that we have in order to attain it. And the pursuit is driven by a desire to fill a bothersome hole in the human heart. Blaise Pascal, the French philosopher, put it this way: "What else does this craving, and this helplessness, proclaim but that there was once in man a true happiness, of which all that now remains is the empty print and trace?"[3] In other words, this longing that we have identified tells us that human beings are born with something missing. We enter this world without the connection to the God who made us; we come into the world with a "God-shaped vacuum" at the center of our life.

THE PURSUIT OF HAPPINESS . . .
IN GOD

John Piper's seminal work, *Desiring God,* makes the compelling argument that God has placed in our hearts the gift of *desire* centered on our pursuit of happiness as the end-all and be-all. Piper quotes Pascal, "All men seek happiness. This is without exception. Whatever different means they employ, they all tend to this end."[4] I used

to make what I now consider a false assertion. Decrying our popular culture's obsession with happiness, I believed that this pursuit of happiness was simply narcissistic, an "it's all about me" way of living. I could be heard to say in sermons, "I'm tired of hearing parents summing up their desire for their children with, 'All I want for them is to be happy [said with sappy sarcasm].'" I would follow this up with the pietistic rant, "God doesn't want us to be happy; he wants us to be holy," as if there was a choice between the two. But Piper has convinced me that God wants us to be happy . . . in him. In fact, we ought to seek our own happiness with our whole heart, with all the passion that can be stirred in us, for then we'll find the true source of happiness, God himself. The line that Piper lives by is, "God is most glorified in me, when I am most satisfied in Him."[5]

In other words, the human problem is not that our passions and desires are too strong, but that they are too weak. Another way to look at the sinful nature of human beings is that we allow our desires to fall short of the God for whom we are made. We try to fill that hole in our heart with that which can never satisfy. C. S. Lewis put it like this: "We are half-hearted creatures, fooling about with drink and sex and ambition when infinite joy is offered to us, like an ignorant child who wants to go on making mud pies in a slum because he cannot imagine what is meant by an offer of a holiday at sea. We are far too easily pleased."[6]

The Lord, speaking through the prophet

Jeremiah, addressed this tendency we have as human beings to exchange what could be truly fulfilling for what can never satisfy: "My people have committed two sins: They have forsaken me, *the spring of living water,* and have dug their own cisterns, *broken cisterns that cannot hold water*" (Jeremiah 2:13). So whether it is trying to fill a God-shaped vacuum with what does not fit or drinking from containers that leak, we fall prey to the false promises of this world that tell us they'll bring the rewards we think we're seeking.

OUR LEAKY CISTERNS

What are the false promises that we fall for? What are the ends we are told will lead us to fullness of life if we pursue them? Here are the some of the short-term pleasures in which we indulge that we foolishly think will bring long-term satisfaction.

1. Material comfort. We seem to be enticed by life's titillating pleasures that so often come in the form of electronic gadgets. The latest one pleases for a while, until, of course, the next one offers the promise of even greater satisfaction. But these are all distractions from deeper lasting fulfillment. John Piper writes, "We have settled for a home, a family, a few friends, a job, a television, a microwave oven, an occasional night out, a yearly vacation and perhaps a new computer."[7] It's not that any of these things in themselves is bad; they're just simply not sufficient. They can't carry the freight for which our hearts are designed. The preacher in Ecclesiastes, after summing up his pursuit of

all that this world has to offer, sadly draws this conclusion: "Yet when I surveyed all that my hands had done and what I had toiled to achieve, everything was meaningless, a chasing after the wind; nothing was gained under the sun" (Ecclesiastes 2:11).[8]

2. Sex and pornography. The epitome of short-term pleasure without long-term satisfaction may be the self-indulgence of pornography. Sitting before a computer and lusting after an airbrushed image of our greatest fantasy allows for momentary sensations to flood our body. Certainly these distractions allow us to forget the incompleteness of real relationships, or a way to divert us from the tensions and frustrations of life, but ultimately they lead us back to the God-shaped vacuum that is still empty. When sexual thrills are the end we seek, we are simply consumers of others, which leaves behind a string of empty relationships.

3. Power or influence. More lives have been wrecked on the shoals of power than perhaps on any other pursuit. Whether it is material power, political power, positional power or intellectual power, its pursuit can be the supreme human aphrodisiac, for power is simply another name for pride—and pride is at the root of all human sin. At its very essence pride is one-upsmanship; it leads us to fundamentally define ourselves in relationship to those with whom we are competing. Ultimately we are in competition with God for the highest position. Was this not the temptation that the serpent dangled before the original couple?[9] As C. S. Lewis has indicated, it is never sufficient to be smart, good-looking or successful; you must be smarter, better looking and more successful than others.[10] Power or pride is inherently corrupting. Once you have it you never want to relinquish it until, eventually, it leads to your own destruction.

The playwright George Bernard Shaw once said, "There are two tragedies in life. One is to lose your heart's desire. The other is to gain it."[11] Why would it be a tragedy to gain our heart's desire? Because we have the propensity to go after those things that, once we get them, certainly cannot satisfy. We arrive at the mountaintop of our pursuits and find that those pursuits are leaky cisterns; they cannot quench the ache inside us. One newscaster discovered this when, after much striving, he reached the top of his profession but then wondered what he had really attained. At age forty-six he reflected, "I'm now at the top of the mountain that I saw as a young man, and it's not snow. It's mostly salt. You see, now I'm ready for the day when I get kicked off that salt-capped mountain. My life was predicated on getting there."[12] His cistern was filled with salt water.

OUR DAMAGED SOULS

All of the above false promises are even more exacerbated if we have grown up with damaged souls. Dallas Willard writes, "There is a developmental order to the soul, such that if it does not receive what it needs to receive within appropriate peri-

ods of time as it grows, its further progression toward wholeness is permanently hindered."[13] If a person grows up in an alcoholic home, for example, or does not receive affection in the formative years, or knows only chaos and insecurity, the soul becomes disordered and starved for affection, and often goes seeking for order and affection in all the wrong places. Whether this damage leads to serial marriages or the inability to make deep human connections, or to some form of physical addiction, the soul is seeking to find that missing something for which it was designed. G. K. Chesterton was quoted as saying that the man who knocks at the door of the brothel is looking for God.

The same psalmist who longed for God as a deer pants for water offered the repeated refrain, "Why are you downcast, O my soul? Why so disturbed within me? Put your hope in God, for I will yet praise him, my Savior and my God" (Psalm 42:5-6, 11; 43:5). Even in the midst of the despondency of despair, the psalmist knew there was a way out. His desire would lead him to the ultimate One who was his hope and the object of his praise.

MADE FOR JOY IN GOD

Like the psalmist, then, we want to allow the desire that God has placed in us to have its full effect and lead us to the One we were made to love and enjoy. The point that John Piper continuously makes in *Desiring God* is that we were made for joy. God is most glorified in us when we are most satisfied in him. Psalm 16 draws this conclusion about God's intent for us: "You will fill me with joy in your presence, with eternal pleasures at your right hand" (Psalm 16:11). It is coming to behold his beauty and wonder that leads to us finding our greatest pleasure.

C. S. Lewis says that this really is the point of praise; we praise what we enjoy. When you see a good movie, for example, you naturally want to tell someone about it, because it's in the telling that you relive your joy. Praise is simply the spontaneous expression of joy toward what has captured our fancy.

Jesus is constantly inviting us to allow God to capture our fancy—to make God the object of our desire—by stirring up that desire for him that he's placed in our souls. You get the sense that the hunger and thirst only get more passionate the more we pursue the God we long to know. In this sense, Matthew 5:6 could be translated as, "Blessed are the hungering and thirsting ones." Though God is the satisfaction for our souls, there is so much of him that our appetites expand as our knowledge of God increases. In other words, hunger and thirst for God do not lead to a place of satisfaction where you never hunger and thirst again. It is, rather, a state of continuous pursuit that only expands our appetite, because there will always be more of God to feast upon.

In Luke 11, in response to the disciples' request that Jesus teach them to pray, Jesus urges them (and us) to seek, ask and knock, because there is a reward in doing so. His repetition only underscores the im-

portance of what he's saying: "So I say to you: Ask and it will be given to you; seek and you will find; knock and the door will be opened to you. For everyone who asks receives; he who seeks finds; and to him who knocks, the door will be opened" (Luke 11:9-10). The present imperative structure of Jesus' language also highlights the intensity of his command: "Ask and keep on asking; seek and keep on seeking; knock and keep on knocking."

Why? You will not be disappointed. You will receive what you ask for; you will find what you are seeking; the door will be opened for those who are knocking. But what is this all about? What is the goal of our asking, seeking and knocking? Jesus immediately goes on to solve the riddle. He tells us that this all leads to the greatest gift that God could give us. He paints the picture of ultimate satisfaction. God is like a father, he tells us, who loves to give good gifts to his children. Even evil and godless parents love their children enough to not give them a snake when they ask for a fish or a scorpion when they ask for an egg, he says, somewhat sarcastically. How much more, then, will your heavenly Father (who is good to the core) "give the Holy Spirit to those who *ask* him!" (Luke 11:13). This is the final "ask," and it's an invitation to ask for the very thing our hearts desire most.

What is this gift of the Holy Spirit? Who is the Holy Spirit? The Holy Spirit is the presence of God living in us! *The greatest gift God can give us is more of himself—* and that's exactly what he offers!

COMING HOME

This leads us to the basic longing that is built into the human soul. We yearn to be known by God, who is Father, and to be embraced as his beloved children. At the moment of Jesus' baptism, just before he is launched into his public ministry, we are allowed to eavesdrop on an intimate exchange between Father and Son. As Jesus emerges from the waters of John's baptism, the Holy Spirit alights on him in the form of a dove, symbolizing the presence and power of God for his mission ahead. And at this moment, the Father has a word for his Son.

I can imagine many things that the Father could have said to his Son right then, knowing the hardship that awaited him along the way and his ultimate rendezvous with the cross. There could have been a little coaching talk: "Go get 'em, Son. I am with you all the way." Or a word of admonition: "Don't let those so and so's get you down." But of all the things that the Father could have said to the Son, he told him simply the place that he has in his heart: "You are my Son, chosen and marked by my love, pride of my life" (Mark 1:11 *The Message*). Even Jesus needed to be sustained with this reminder of who he was. This serves as the paradigm of the kind of relationship we can have with the Father.

To love God with all of our soul means that we find our satisfaction in the One we come to know as Father. We long for a Father who takes pleasure and delight in us, serves as our protector against life's harm,

provides wise counsel in the midst of life's complexities, is patient with our missteps, and tells us that he will never leave us or forsake us. When we come to rest in this Father—our heavenly Father—our hearts arrive at home. Indeed, the apostle John tells us we are home when we can affirm, "How great is the love the Father has lavished on us, that we should be called children of God! And that is what we are!" (1 John 3:1).

Jesus offered this invitation to those worn-out travelers along the way: "Come to me, all you who are weary and burdened, and I will give you rest. Take my yoke upon you and learn from me, for I am gentle and humble in heart, and you will find *rest for your souls*. For my yoke is easy and my burden is light" (Matthew 11:28-30). Richard Foster paints a wonderful picture of this in his book *Prayer: Finding the Heart's True Home*. He tells the story of a friend who was walking through a shopping mall with his two-year-old son. On that day his son was in a particularly cantankerous mood, fussing and fuming. The father tried everything he could to quiet his son, but nothing seemed to work. Then, under a special inspiration, it seemed, the father scooped up his son and, holding him to his chest, began singing an impromptu love song. None of the words rhymed and he sang off-key, as if he were singing an awkward chant. "I love you," he intoned. "I'm so glad you're my boy. You make me happy. I like the way you laugh." On they went from one store to the next. The father continued to sing off-key, making up words that did not rhyme. The child began to relax and became still, listening to this strange and wonderful song. After they finished their shopping, as the father was preparing to buckle his son into his car seat, the child lifted his head and said simply, "Sing it to me again, Daddy! Sing it to me again."

Hunger. Thirst. Seek. Ask. Knock. "Sing it to me again, Daddy." Maybe this is what Jesus meant when he said, "Let the little children come to me . . . for the kingdom of God belongs to such as these" (Mark 10:14).

May this prayer of A. W. Tozer sum up the desire of our hearts:

O God, I have tasted Thy goodness, and it has both satisfied me and made me thirsty for more. I am painfully conscious of my need of further grace. I am ashamed of my lack of desire. O God, the triune God, I want to want Thee; I long to be filled with longing; I thirst to be made more thirsty still. Show me Thy glory, I pray Thee, that so I may know Thee indeed. Begin in mercy a new work of love within me. Say to my soul, "Rise up, my love, my fair one, and come away." Then give me grace to rise and follow Thee up from this misty lowland where I have wandered so long. In Jesus' name, Amen.[14]

---

[1]It's true that *heart, soul* and *spirit* can be used somewhat interchangeably to describe this deep longing to connect with God (see Isaiah 26:8-9). For our purposes, we'll use the word *soul,* which is often identified as the place of our deepest feelings of desire and hope.

[2]"As the Deer" by Marty Mystrom and "O God, You Are My God" by Fernando Ortega.

[3]Pascal is often quoted as saying, "There is a God shaped vacuum in the heart of every man which cannot be filled by any created thing, but only by God, the Creator, made known through Jesus." The problem is that this quote cannot be found. The one closest to it is the one quoted above in Pascal's *Pensees* 7.425.

[4]John Piper, *Desiring God* (Sisters, Ore.: Multnomah, 2003), p. 19.

[5]Ibid., p. 10.

[6]C. S. Lewis, *The Weight of Glory and Other Addresses* (Grand Rapids: Eerdmans, 1965), pp. 1-2.

[7]Piper, *Desiring God,* p. 99.

[8]Read Ecclesiastes 2:1-11. There is no better description of the vain pursuit of things and their ultimate disappointment than what you will read here.

[9]Genesis 3:1-5 is a masterful depiction of the human heart in competition with God. Adam and Eve were told by the serpent that God's intentions could not be trusted because he was simply protecting his position of authority.

[10]C. S. Lewis, *Mere Christianity* (New York: Macmillan, 1943), p. 110.

[11]George Bernard Shaw, *Man and Superman,* act 4.

[12]Gail Sheehy, *Passages* (New York: Bantam, 1976), p. 173.

[13]Dallas Willard, *Renovation of the Heart* (Colorado Springs: NavPress, 2002), p. 201.

[14]Warren Wiersbe, ed., *The Best of A. W. Tozer* (Grand Rapids: Baker, 1978), p. 19.

Reading Study Guide

1. How would you describe the hunger and thirst for God that's in the human soul?

   Do you see evidence of this in yourself and in the people you share life with? Describe.

2. Do you agree or disagree with the statement, "All people seek happiness as their strongest pursuit in life"?

   How can this pursuit for happiness actually lead us to God?

3. Human beings seem to be distracted by the pursuit of things in life that cannot truly bring satisfaction. Why do you think this is?

   What other false pursuits do you see besides the ones mentioned in the reading?

4. On a scale of one to ten, with one being a very low appetite and ten being a ravenous appetite, where would you place yourself in your hunger and thirst for God? Explain.

5. The reading asserts that our deepest longing is to come to know God as our Father. What does this mean to you? Where are you on that quest?

6. Write your own prayer stating what you want your heart's desire to be in order to love God with all of your soul.

Going Deeper

Piper, John. *Desiring God: Meditations of a Christian Hedonist.* Sisters, Ore.: Multnomah, 2003. Piper rewrites the first answer to the first question in the Westminster Catechism by changing one word. Q: "What is the chief end of man?" A: "The chief end of man is to love God [by] enjoy[ing] Him forever." There is the greatest of rewards in the pursuit of God, Piper tells us, and that is joy. He also emphasizes that God never intended for us to seek him without a reward and that it's not wrong to pursue God to find our joy; Piper asserts that that's actually God's intent.

5 / A Soul . . . Fully Alive . . .
to the Glory of God

LOOKING AHEAD

MEMORY VERSES: Galatians 6:4-5 *(The Message)*
BIBLE STUDY: Psalm 139:1-18
READING: We Find Our Souls in Christ

 Core Truth

What does it mean to be soulful beings?

As people we do not have souls; we are souls. The soul does not exist as some compartment in our life, separate and distinct from body, mind and spirit. Our soulfulness is the integration of these three aspects into one personality, which is the unique expression of who God has created us to be. We love God with all of our soul when we present our personality to him so that we can become the distinct characters in God's drama we were intended to be.

1. Identify key words or phrases in the question and answer above, and state their meaning in your own words.

2. Restate the core truth in your own words.

3. What questions or issues does the core truth raise for you?

Memory Verse Study Guide

There is an old Quaker saying, "All He has is thee." In other words, the Lord has tied the accomplishment of his purposes to the people he has made. He made sure that there is quite a variety of "souls" that cover the waterfront of gifts, abilities, temperaments, interests, passions and so forth. It is our responsibility to sense the tone and tenor of our soul in order to be the best "me" we can be.

For our memory verse this week, I have chosen to use Eugene Peterson's translation, because he captures the heart of this discovery and deployment of what God has placed into our makeup.

1. *Putting it in context:* Galatians 6:1-3 in *The Message* translation says, "Live creatively, friends. If someone falls into sin, forgivingly restore him, saving your critical comments for yourself. You might be needing forgiveness before the day's out. Stoop down and reach out to those who are oppressed. Share their burdens, and so complete Christ's law. If you think you are too good for that, you are badly deceived." What is to be the spirit or attitude of a person who lovingly assists someone who has fallen into sin?

2. The memory verses are *Galatians 6:4-5:* "Make a careful exploration of who you are and the work you have been given, and then sink yourself into that. Don't be impressed with yourself. Don't compare yourself with others. Each of you must take responsibility for doing the creative best you can with your own life" *(The Message)*. In light of verses 1-3, what do you think it means to "make a careful exploration of who you are"?

3. What is the connection between "who you are" and "the work you have been given" to do?

4. What would it look like in your own context and life for you to "sink yourself"—to really bring all of who you are—into the work that you've been given to do?

What distracts you from this focus?

5. What is the danger of comparing yourself with others?

6. What is required of you to "take responsibility for doing [your] creative best"?

What excuses do you find yourself making for not "taking responsibility"?

Inductive Bible Study Guide

C. S. Lewis has written, "I read in a periodical the other day that the fundamental thing is how we think of God. By God Himself, it is not! How God thinks of us is not only more important, but infinitely more important."[1] How does God view us? Where do we fit into his heart? Are we known by him? These are the questions that our text addresses.

1. *Read Psalm 139:1-18.* This psalm of David divides neatly into two sections: verses 1-12 and verses 13-18. How would you describe the connection between these two sections?

2. According to verses 1-6, what does God know about us?

3. Looking at verses 7-12, what are the different ways that David might try to flee God?

   What does David conclude?

4. How is David affected by his reflections on God in these first twelve verses?

5. In verses 13-18, what images does David use to describe the wonder of his own creation?

6. When David is viewed from God's standpoint, what does God see?

7. What are the implications of this description of the uniqueness of every person created by God? What message is conveyed in this text?

👓 Reading: We Find Our Souls in Christ

In our first section on loving God with all of our soul we looked at one dimension of how the soul is pictured in Scripture: as our deepest longings, desires, affections, hopes and dreams. And we asserted that it's from this realm—from within the recesses of our being—that our aspirations surface. The Scriptures analogize these interior stirrings to the physical drive to satisfy hunger and thirst; to know and be known by the One who placed his image within us, we saw, is a universal craving. We also looked at how our souls are finally at rest—at home—when we can call God our Father and accept that we are embraced as his beloved children. Finally, we closed the last chapter with a prayer from A. W. Tozer, asking God to create a yearning for him that is so passionate that it could never be fully satisfied in this life.

In this reading we want to explore another dimension of what it means to love God with all our soul. Quite frankly, I have generally found the nature of the soul elusive. It seems to be nebulous and shapeless, like an eerie mist that we cannot get a hold on. When we consider our heart, mind and strength, it is far easier to be concrete because we can associate each with an aspect of our physical makeup: the heart is the central organ in our bodies, the mind is the nerve center of the brain, and our strength is the energy of our physical bodies. But what is the soul? Where does the soul reside?

Popular wisdom seems to associate the soul with some ghostly entity that survives death and is eternal. We have, inadvertently, I believe, adopted more of a Greek understanding of the soul than a Christian or biblical perspective. The Greeks viewed the soul as a separate, eternal unit that was trapped inside the human body. The body was simply the encasing that served as a prison house for the soul. At death the body was discarded so that the soul could be released to enter the everlasting realm.

Yet biblically it is far more accurate to say that we *are* souls than that we *have* a soul. To say we have a soul seems to locate the soul in some unlocatable compartment within us. But to say that we are souls means that being a soul defines us and permeates our entire personhood.

In this reading, then, we'll look at how the soul, biblically, is to be equated with our self: our individuality, our personhood, even our personality. We love God with all of our soul by becoming, as fully as possible, the unique persons that God created and redeemed us to be.

WE ARE SOULS

Human beings created in the image of God are soulful beings. The Bible describes the creation of Adam as a merging of the physical with the spiritual: "The LORD God formed the man from the dust of the ground and breathed into his nostrils the breath [soul] of life, and the man became a living being" (Genesis 2:7). Thus, the soul integrates the heart, mind and body into a human personality. In other words, the soul refers not to one entity within the person but to the entirety of who a person is.

Early in my Christian walk I used to hear people refer to witnessing or evangelism as "soul winning." That phrase always rubbed me the wrong way. "Soul winning" seemed to be concerned only about snatching people from the fires of hell, claiming them for eternity, with little concern for the condition of the whole person now. Yet in the best sense of that phrase, "soul winning" does mean redeeming the entire person—heart, mind and body—in order to become the full persons God intended.

In the New Testament, the Greek word for "soul"—*psyche*—is equated with the individual, the self, life or personhood. We immediately recognize the word as the root of *psych*ology. In fact, the discipline of psychology is quite literally the "study of the soul." Jesus used the word *psyche* when he pointed the way to the fullness of life. Note how his words take on new meaning when we insert the word *soul* for *life:* "For whoever wants to save his life [*psyche,* soul] will lose it, but whoever loses his life [*psyche,* soul] for me and for the gospel will save it" (Mark 8:35). Is Jesus only concerned here with our eternal destiny? Is he only concerned about our future existence? No. Jesus equates the individual life with the soul and the totality of what it means to be human.

The truth is, we are all souls heading in one direction or another. We are immor-

tal beings with two possible destinations. The trajectory we choose is what makes the difference. The way to life in the present moment and forevermore is by losing our self into Christ, for then we find our true self. Another Greek word, *zoe,* helps us understand this kind of life—life that enters into the *psyche* and truly brings us soulful beings alive. It's the life Jesus was referring to when he said, "I have come that they may have *life [zoe],* and have it to the full" (John 10:10). This life *(zoe)* is always associated with Jesus as the source; only he can give it. As Jesus said of himself, "I am the bread of *life [zoe].* He who comes to me will never go hungry, and he who believes in me will never be thirsty" (John 6:35).

In our natural, soulful state we have immortal life but not eternal life. *Zoe* is the life that comes to us from outside our soulfulness; it's most often translated as "eternal life"—and that eternal life begins in the here and now and continues into an eternal future. In Nicodemus and Jesus' nighttime conversation, Jesus told him that he must be born again or born from above. He then summed up this life offered to Nicodemus with these familiar words: "For God so loved the world that he gave his one and only Son, that whoever believes in him shall not perish but have eternal life *[zoe]*" (John 3:16). Where is this life found? In relationship with Jesus. Eternal life is not equated biblically with the state we enter into when we die; it is, as Jesus himself defines it, what we receive in connection to Jesus, in relationship with him: "Now this is eternal life *[zoe]:* that they may know you [the Father], the only true God, and Jesus Christ, whom you have sent" (John 17:3).

We are, as I've noted, all souls *(psyche);* the goal of this life, though, is to be souls *(psyche) alive with Jesus-life (zoe).* Before we can really dive into what this looks like in practice, though—what it means to really love God with our unique personality—we need to consider a few facts about the nature of personality itself.

THE MYSTERY OF PERSONALITY

Personality is very difficult to define, even for professional psychologists. James Beck, a psychologist and professor, writes, "Human personality almost defies description. . . . The term *personality* . . . refers to those emotional and psychological features of our immaterial selves that influence and indeed govern how we relate to others. No one is able to draw a line around the personality and define it with great precision."[2] We can attempt to describe personality through various factors or schemes (see below), but we can't reduce it to these factors. There is always something more; there is a mystery about what makes us human, and we simply can't explain how our personality—our soul—integrates heart, mind and body into the one-of-a-kind person that we are.

We live at a time when we are searching for ways to capture the uniqueness of the individual. In our psychological age, with a focus on what makes the individual tick, a myriad of inventories have

been developed to define more concretely what makes up our personality. The following is just a partial list of the ones I've taken to understand the mystery of me: the Myers Briggs Type Indicator, which helps you identify your personality type out of sixteen possible types; the Taylor-Johnson Temperament Analysis, which measures nine polar opposite traits; the Gallup StrengthsFinder assessment, which covers thirty-five strengths and helps you identify your top five; the DiSC profile, which measures four aspects of behavior (Dominance, Influence, Steadiness, Conscientiousness); and the Enneagram, which identifies nine personality types and helps you define and recognize your true and false self. The list goes on. But what do all these inventories have in common? What is their intent? Each one, from its own angle, is attempting to get at the essence of the unique persons that we are, with the underlying message of, "Be who you were designed to be. Accept your temperament. Build on your God-given attributes. Find joy by fulfilling your purpose."

This message, however, might raise more questions for us. How do we be who we're designed to be while also "losing our life" for Christ's sake (see Mark 8:35)? The answer is another mystery: Our fullness of life or personhood actually awaits us in Christ. As David Benner says, "Paradoxically, as we become more and more like Christ we become more uniquely our own true self."[3]

C. S. Lewis has a profound discussion of

this very issue at the end of his classic *Mere Christianity*. His reflections on personality come under the broader heading of what it means to be the "new man"—to be transformed into the image and likeness of Jesus. When Jesus says that we find our life by losing our life for his sake, it may seem like he is, in fact, asking us to deny our uniqueness or our individuality. To demonstrate that just the opposite is true, Lewis uses a homespun illustration. He asks us to suppose that there are people who have never tasted salt. Once they've tried a pinch of salt by itself, we mention to them that we put this tangy substance on our food. Their first thought might be, *Then everything will taste like salt. Salt will cancel out all other flavors.* Yet we know that the opposite is the case. The purpose of this spice, when used in the right proportions, is to draw out the inherent flavor of our meats, eggs, vegetables and other foods. Salt enhances rather than dominates the flavor of the food.

So it is with Christ. Lewis goes on to say that when we try to live our lives on our own apart from Christ (in other words, we try to "save our life"), we simply end up conforming ourselves to the prevailing standards and expectations of the world, thereby becoming dull cookie-cutter versions of everyone else.

> The more we get what we now call "ourselves" out of the way and let Him [Christ] take us over, the more truly ourselves we become. There is so much of Him that millions and millions of "little Christs," all different, will still be too few to express Him fully. He made them all. He invented—as an author invents characters in a novel—all the different men [and women] that you and I were intended to be. In that sense our real selves are all waiting for us in Him. . . . It is when I turn to Christ, when I give myself up to His Personality, that I first begin to have a real personality of my own.[4]

Jesus tells us that it is in giving up that we get. The greatest rewards are held out for those who exchange the running of their life for the relinquishing of their life for Christ's sake. We actually lose nothing in the abandonment of self; it is only then that we find our true self. Lewis points out that this losing to gain is the natural rhythm in all things of value. In social settings, for example, if you want to make a good impression on others, you have to stop thinking about what impression you are making. If you're overly self-conscious, you're likely undermining the very thing you desire. Similarly, in writing, if I try to be creative or original, I'll most likely end up simply copying someone else's style. If, however, I tell the truth as I know it through the distinct personality and thought structure God has given me, then I will be my most creative.

GOD'S WILL WITHIN

If the soul is the unique self designed by God—and then surrendered to him by us—to play a part in his drama, it would seem that discovering this part is one of the primary ways that we love God. So we naturally ask, what is my purpose? What do I have to offer to the world? What am I made to do? In other words, what is God's will for my life? I would assert that *much of the will of God for you is written into you.* In other words, looking within and being a steward of your spiritual gifts, your natural talents, your intentions and your desires is a primary way we discover what God's desire is for us.

But is it wrong to focus on the self? Is this being selfish? Dr. David Benner, a psychologist, spiritual director and former professor of psychology and spirituality, often asked his students, "What would you identify as the most important thing for your existence and well-being?" Being well-trained, his students would give what sounds like the theologically correct answer: some form of finding and serving God, without any reference to the self. Yet the great theologians have always understood that we must serve God by *discovering* our unique self. John Calvin commences his magnum opus, *Institutes of the Christian Religion,* with, "There is no deep knowing of God without a deep knowing of self and no deep knowing of self without a deep knowing of God." Likewise, Augustine prayed, "Grant, Lord, that I may know myself that I may know Thee."

One of the ways that we know God is by knowing the self that God has made. Again, much of the will of God for us is written into us. The will of God is generally not some elusive something out there

that he circumstantially leads us into; it is being a steward of what God has placed into the package that we call the soulful person. We get to simply unwrap the gift of ourselves to be used for the glory of God. As we discovered in the "Memory Verse Study Guide" for this chapter, Eugene Peterson's translation of Galatians 6:4-5 captures well the task ahead for us: "Make a careful exploration of who you are and the work you have been given, and then sink yourself into that. Don't be impressed with yourself. Don't compare yourself with others. Each of you must take responsibility for doing the creative best you can with your own life" *(The Message).*

I can think of no better commentary on this verse than David Benner's reflections in his book *The Gift of Being Yourself:*

> Without deemphasizing the value of the Bible in knowing my calling, I have come to understand an even more basic place in which God's will for me has been communicated. That is in the givens of my being. My temperament, my personality, my abilities, and my interests and passions all say something about who I was called to be, not simply who I am. If I really believe that I was created by God and invited to find my place in his kingdom, I have to take seriously what God has already revealed about who I am.[5]

OUR CONSISTENT DESIGN

What we will find in this discovery of who

we are is that we are amazingly consistent in our design throughout our life. We have a personality that is recognizable because we are the same people day in and day out. Beyond our physical characteristics that distinguish us from others, we are an amalgam of temperament, tone of voice, mannerisms, nervous ticks and ways of doing things that defines our personhood. Because of this, we do not wake up each day as people of unlimited possibilities, as if overnight the molecules in our bodies rearranged themselves so that today we could be a concert pianist or a nuclear physicist whereas yesterday we were oriented to be a writer of mystery novels or an elementary school teacher. This is part of the mystery of our personality or psyche as soulful beings. There is an inner rudder that guides us.

Let me use my own wife as an illustration of this consistent design. Because of the way my wife is wired, she will shape her physical environment to suit her creative image of beauty and functionality. This is just in her. No one has to make her do it; it simply emerges from within who she is. I don't have to ask her to spend some time thinking about how she would want to improve the physical quality of our home. She'll just do this as naturally as eating. Once she gets in her mind some changes she thinks would improve our home's appearance, value, comfort or usefulness, she thinks it through, researches it, and then comes to me and says, "This is what we should do." Early in our marriage, I guess I thought it was my job to

throw cold water on any of her initiatives. After all, they cost money. And since I was such a careful and cautious steward of the resources God had given us, I could always think of more compassionate—rather than "selfish"—reasons for spending that money (my own book budget excluded, of course). Then I came to realize two things. First, once my wife had decided something, it was far better to acquiesce. She was going to win anyway. But second, and far more important, these decisions were an expression of a creative vision that God had planted in her. I was thwarting the very essence of the way my wife was created to be. (And by the way, she always made very good decisions within the parameters of our financial situation at the time.)

A Helpful Approach to Self-Discovery

I have already referenced some very helpful approaches to discerning how God has wired us as a way to understand God's purpose. Each of these assessments has its value. But the one I personally have found most beneficial is SIMA (System for Identifying Motivated Abilities), which is based on observing the patterns in our personal story and noticing a major theme from the *motivated abilities* that run through the dimensions of our life. To start this process you would divide your life into four age segments and then ask yourself, for each segment, "What accomplishments gave me the most personal satisfaction?" This is not necessarily about successes, because we cannot all be successful. This is also not about accolades that have come from your family of origin, or the values of your community, or what our culture celebrates as rewards. Beyond success and other people's affirmation, what has resonated deep within you and been personally satisfying, so that you would say of it, "I was created for this"? The answer to this question gets to the soulfulness of the individual.

This deep motivation or intention is what God has placed in our heart. Ralph Mattson and Arthur Miller refer to this as the shape of our will.[6] There is a consistency to us that is rather remarkable. Mattson and Miller state that the pattern is the same throughout our life—before and after Christ:

> Our evidence demonstrates that motivational patterns do not change when a person becomes a Christian. The ingredients seen prior to conversion are seen after conversion. This is disturbing to people who expect otherwise, but perhaps we will better understand our position in Christ if we see that God's intention for us is not replacement of who we are, but redemption of who we are. God's creation of us, including our basic motivation pattern, is not bad. . . . Redemption means bringing us back to that which God originally intended. . . . Conversion has us rejoicing in the fact that we are enabled to become who we originally were made to be, rather than becoming someone entirely different.[7]

The apostle Paul is exhibit A for the above truth. Did Paul's personality change after he became a believer? Was he not amazingly consistent in his passionate pursuit of the truth? In his redemption he pursued a different understanding of the truth than he did prior to conversion, but he was the same firebrand; the difference was that he was now controlled by love, and was therefore fulfilling the purpose for which he was originally made.

OUR UNIQUE MOTIVATION

When I reflect on the accomplishments that have been the most personally satisfying for me, I can see what's been my core motivation: I am motivated to have a shaping influence and impact on forming people in their Christian faith through personal relationship, and through the transformation of their thinking through teaching and writing which illuminates God's Word. I have no greater joy than seeing people come alive to their potential as the people God has created them to be both individually and as part of a team working toward a larger purpose. When, then, am I most alive to the glory of God?

- When I am sitting face to face with two-to-three other men around the truth of God's Word and we are sharing our lives deeply with each other.

- When I am studying God's Word in order to provide practical teaching that will shape the minds and hearts of God's people.

- When I am teaching about how disciples are made biblically and practically.

• When I am trying to tackle difficult projects (like this one) in order to make the complex simple and understandable for others.

• When I am affirming the gifts and contributions of others in the context of being on a team that's working together to fulfill a mission that is greater than any of us could do on our own.

What accomplishments in your life have brought the most satisfaction to you? When have you sensed, "I was created for this!"?

We love God with all of our soul when we relinquish our life to Christ in order to become the unique characters in God's drama that we were intended to be. The story of Rabbi Zusya is a dramatic illustration of this. Rabbi Zusya embodied for his students a man who loved God with all his heart and soul, and he demonstrated this in his generous life. One day Rabbi Zusya did not show up at his House of Study. The worried students finally rushed to his house that evening to find the rabbi in a very weakened state. His students cried

out, "Rabbi Zusya, what has happened? How can we help you?"

The rabbi replied, "There is nothing you can do. I'm dying and I am very frightened."

The students were shocked that the rabbi was frightened. "Did you not teach us that all living things die?"

Yes, the rabbi affirmed what they had learned.

"Then why are you afraid? You have led such a good life. You have believed in God with a faith as strong as Abraham's and you have followed the commandments as carefully as Moses."

"Thank you. But this is not why I am afraid," explained the rabbi. "For if God should ask me why I did not act like Abraham, I can say that I was not Abraham. And if God asks me why I did not act like Moses, I can also say that I was not Moses. But if God should ask me to account for the times when I did not act like Zusya, what shall I say then?"[8]

To love God with all your soul is to be what the early church father Irenaeus declared: *"Man fully alive is the glory of God."*[9] This is what it means to be a soulful person.

---

[1]C. S. Lewis, *The Weight of Glory and Other Addresses* (Grand Rapids: Eerdmans, 1965), p. 13.

[2]James Beck, *Jesus and Personality Theory: Exploring the Five-Factor Model* (Downers Grove, Ill.: InterVarsity Press, 1999), pp. 17-18.

[3]David Benner, *The Gift of Being Yourself: The Sacred Call to Self-Discovery* (Downers Grove, Ill.: InterVarsity Press, 2004), p. 16.

[4]C. S. Lewis, *Mere Christianity* (New York: Macmillan, 1943), p. 190.

[5]Benner, *Gift of Being Yourself,* p. 101.

[6]Ralph Mattson and Arthur F. Miller have written two excellent books that explore how to find our motivated abilities: *Finding a Job You Can Love* (Phillipsburg, N.J.: P & R Publishing, 1999) and *The Truth About You* (Berkeley, Calif.: Ten Speed Press, 1989).

[7]Mattson and Arthur Miller, *Finding a Job You Can Love,* p. 119.

[8]Gila Gevirtz, *Partners with God* (Springfield, N.J.: Behrman House, 1995), pp. 80-82.

[9]Irenaeus, *Against Heresies* 4.20.

Reading Study Guide

1. What comes to your mind when you think of the soul?

2. Do you agree or disagree that general discussions of the soul often leave us with a "nebulous and shapeless" understanding that is very hard to get our minds around? Why?

3. Trace the line of reasoning that shows how, biblically, the soul can be equated with our individuality or personality.

   What do you think of this argument?

4. What is the relationship between the *psyche* (soul) and *zoe* (life)?

5. Explain how it is that only when we lose ourselves to Christ do we actually find ourselves.

6. What is the meaning of the sentence, "Much of the will of God for you is written into you"?

7. Have you taken any "personality inventories"? In what ways were they helpful? In what ways were they unhelpful?

8. How would you answer the question, "What accomplishments in my life gave me the most personal satisfaction?" (Suggestion: Divide your life into four equal age segments and answer this question for each of these periods of time.)

What consistent pattern of motivation and satisfaction did you notice?

Going Deeper

Lucado, Max. *Cure for the Common Life: Living in Your Sweet Spot.* Nashville: Thomas Nelson, 2005. Lucado includes a Sweet Spot Discovery Guide as an appendix to his book. It takes you into the People Management International, Inc., approach to SIMA as developed by Ralph Mattson and Arthur Miller. The extensive exercises included in the book delve far more fully into this self-discovery process than this study can. It is highly recommended that you take the time to do the hard work of uncovering the mystery of yourself so that you can be a faithful steward of the design God has placed in you.

Part Three

LOVE THE LORD YOUR GOD . . .
WITH ALL YOUR MIND

The mind is perhaps the most powerful instrument that God has given us. For it is through our minds that we see life. We don't see with our eyes. We see with our minds. This may have been what Jesus meant when he said, "The eye is the lamp of the body. If your eyes are good, your whole body will be full of light. But if your eyes are bad, your whole body will be full of darkness. If then the light within is darkness, how great is that darkness" (Matthew 6:22-23). Jesus builds off the obvious physical truth about the clarity of our eyes and the amount of light that is allowed into our bodies.

What determines our seeing? The apostle Paul clearly locates our ability to see in our minds or our thinking. "Do not conform any longer to the pattern of this world, but be transformed by the renewing of your *mind*. Then you will be able to test and approve what God's will is—his good, pleasing and perfect will" (Romans 12:2). Paul locates the work of transformation into Christlikeness in our thinking or perceiving. He reminds the Ephesians of the distorted thinking in which they were immersed before they learned a new way of life in Christ (Ephesians 4:20-22). "So I tell you this, and insist on it in the Lord, that you must no longer live as the Gentiles do, in the futility of their *thinking*. They are darkened in their *understanding* and separated from the life of God because of the *ignorance* that is in them due to the hardening of their hearts" (Ephesians 4:17-18).

In lesson six we will explore the fundamental way that the apostle Paul viewed life, as one with a *transformed mind*. Paul seemed to see life quite differently than we do. We will try to grasp his perspective and see life through his eyes. We will see that Paul could rejoice in all circumstances. He lived in a way that changing circumstances, positive or negative, did not throw him off kilter. His life did not rise and fall when things were going well or when setbacks came his direction. In this lesson we will explore the "secret" Paul says he discovered so that he was able to be anxious in nothing, but live with a settled peace that passed human comprehension.

Then in lesson seven we will peer more deeply into the *mind's makeup*. Since the mind is the filter through which we see life, we want to know what makes up that filter. In a sense, growing to love God is cleaning up the filter in order to see life through the death and resurrection of Jesus as the decisive events that shape our thinking. What we don't often understand is that the quality of our life, our emotional life, is directly related to our thinking. We never have a feeling, either positive or negative, that has not been preceded by a thought that has triggered the feeling. If the quality of our life is experienced through our emotional climate, then controlling our thought processes can lead us to a place of joy, love and serenity. This is part of the "abundant life" that Jesus said he came to bring us (John 10:10).

6 / Having the Mind of Christ

LOOKING AHEAD

MEMORY VERSES: Mark 10:42-45
BIBLE STUDY: Colossians 3:1-17
READING: Putting on the Mind of Christ

 Core Truth

What does it mean to love God with all of your mind?

Since the mind is the lens through which we see life, it is imperative that the mind be cleansed of falsehood. The Scriptures start with the fact that our minds have been distorted because of our refusal to acknowledge God as the ultimate reality, which in turn has led to false assumptions about life. We love God with our minds by absorbing the truth about who God is as revealed in Scripture and aligning our lives accordingly; in other words, it is through the absorption of Scripture into our way of thinking that we take on the mind of Christ.

1. Identify key words or phrases in the question and answer above, and state their meaning in your own words.

2. Restate the core truth in your own words.

3. What questions or issues does the core truth raise for you?

Memory Verse Study Guide

Much of the ministry of Jesus with his disciples was helping them get their heads screwed on straight. When Jesus called them to follow him, they brought with them the worldly values and perspective into which their life had been immersed. Our memory verses point to one confrontational conversation in which Jesus clearly identifies that their way of thinking or seeing reality was out of step with the value system of the kingdom of God. The disciples needed to adopt a new way of looking at greatness, because their leader viewed greatness as servanthood—even unto death.

1. *Putting it in context:* Read Mark 10:35-41. What was the mindset that led James and John to request a special position when they were with Jesus in his glory? How did this affect the other ten disciples?

2. The memory verses are *Mark 10:42-45*. Copy the verses verbatim.

3. In verse 42, how does Jesus summarize the view of power and authority that was serving as the model for the disciples?

4. According to verses 43-44, what is the view of power and authority that Jesus seeks to put in place of the worldly model?

5. What change of thinking does this require for you? In what specific situations can you see yourself living this out?

6. What feelings surface within you as you contemplate adopting this way of thinking?

7. In verse 45, how does Jesus use himself as the final argument for his position? How did Jesus' view of his identity and role work itself out in his life and ministry?

8. What motivation does this provide for you to adopt this "new mind in Christ"?

Inductive Bible Study Guide

The apostle Paul views the transformation of our minds as a core issue for our growing up in Christ. In the Scripture passage we're going to study here, Paul mixes his images. On the one hand he speaks of where we set our gaze or direct our thoughts, but then he speaks of the clothing or the wardrobe we are to put on. Enjoy the delicious contrast in the qualities between the old and new way of life that is ours in Christ.

1. *Read Colossians 3:1-17.* In verses 1-4, Paul lays out some of the fundamentals for this new way of life that we have in Christ. In your own language, restate his reasons for a dramatic shift.

2. In verses 5-9, Paul catalogs the desires and practices that came with "the life you once lived." Look carefully at the lists in verses 5-6 and 8-9.

   What do the characteristics and practices listed in verses 5-6 have in common?

   What do the characteristics and practices listed in verses 8-9 have in common?

3. How does Paul's description of our "earthly nature" fit with what you've seen and experienced in your life?

4. According to verse 10, what is the basis for the new way of life Paul describes?

5. Paul says that one result of "putting on the new self" is a social equality (v. 11). What are some implications of that?

6. In verses 12-14, Paul describes the new attire we are to put on. As you read this description, how would you summarize what the renewed life looks like?

7. Finally, in verses 15-17 the dominant note that Paul sounds appears to be one of gratitude or thanksgiving (note the repetition). Why might gratitude be the dominant result of the mind that's "set . . . on things above"?

8. As you look at Paul's complete description of the new life in Christ (vv. 12-17), what attire do you need to complete your new wardrobe?

Reading: Putting on the Mind of Christ

The apostle Paul locates transformation into Christlikeness in the mind, exhorting us to "be transformed by the *renewing of [our] mind*" (Romans 12:2). It's the mind that needs a different grid or vantage point from which to view life.

Scripture starts with the assumption that we have much work to do. Learning to walk with Christ means continuously bringing our out-of-phase thinking in line with the reality of God's revelation of himself in Christ. We need a complete transformation from within. In other words, each one of us is a reclamation project and God is in the salvage business.

THE NATURE OF TRANSFORMATION

Let me illustrate reclamation through a personal recollection. During my growing-up years, I watched a dramatic transformation take place. Scholl Canyon in the Southern California community in which I was raised was a gorge where the trash trucks daily unloaded their rotting garbage and human discards. Yet in my twenties I had the opportunity to play golf on this same site. It had been transformed from a stinking landfill into a beautifully manicured green playground overlooking the San Fernando Valley in the Los Angeles Basin. Once the ravine was filled to capacity it was *changed* from a refuse depository into a new creation—or perhaps I should say a place of *re-creation*.

When Paul asserts the need for the transformation—the re-creation—of our minds, he uses language that is quite informative. Romans 12:2 in the Greek, for example, uses two different words for *form*. The first one is *schema,* which is the root of "conform," from which we get the word *scheme*. This word refers to the external, changeable form. So when Paul instructs, "Do not con*form* any longer to the pattern of this world," he's essentially saying, "Don't simply act like a chameleon that adapts to the flora and fauna and becomes indistinguishable from its surroundings." The old Phillips translation captured this in a memorable fashion: "Don't let the world around you *squeeze* you into its own mold."

Paul then says, in contrast, that we are to be "transformed." The root here is different from the root of "conform" *(schema).* It is *morphe,* from which we get the popular word *morph* (in the sense of, for example, seeing computer-generated images *morphing* from a man's to a woman's face). The literal translation of the Greek word here is "metamorphosis." It has to do with becoming a new you from the inside out—a new, unchangeable inner character. Whereas *schema* is adapting to the fleeting fashion and current fads of this world's thinking, *metamorphosis* is a dramatic change—as dramatic as the change of a caterpillar to a butterfly. The caterpillar spins the cocoon and from the chrysalis comes a new being, a butterfly. This is a striking way of saying that our minds need an entirely new way of looking at life.

When I described the transformation of Scholl Canyon from a landfill to a golf course, I didn't tell you the whole story. I did play golf on this "transformed" course, but only one time. Why? Emanating from below the thin layer of topsoil was a nauseating stench. All I could think of when I was standing on the putting green was that my shoes were in touch with a bubbling chemical cauldron. You see, the landfill had been *schematized* (changed on the surface), but it had not *morphed* (changed from deep within). The old garbage had not been removed but just covered over. For a real transformation to occur, the garbage has to be taken out and replaced with *clean* soil. (Sorry; I guess all analogies break down at some point!)

If we are to learn *to love God with all our mind* it is helpful to get a glimpse of what a transformed mind looks like. In the apostle Paul we see such an example. In fact, in one of his letters to the Corinthians he confidently states, "We have the mind of Christ" (1 Corinthians 2:16). What does this look like? Paul shows us, through his life of faith and his writings, what it means to live as one who has adopted the mind of Christ.

As I have tried to get inside Paul's mindset, to look at life through his eyes, I have come to believe that his outlook seems 180 degrees out of phase with our contemporary worldview. Frankly, I think we just don't get what makes Paul tick.

THE SECRET OF CONTENTMENT

The apostle Paul says one of the most truly astounding things that has ever been written: "I have learned the secret of being content in any and every situation, whether well fed or hungry, whether living in plenty or in want. I can do everything through him who gives me strength" (Philippians 4:12-13). If Paul had written this while stretched out on a lounge chair on a Hawaiian white-sand beach, we could cynically reject his assertion. But this letter to the Philippians was most likely written while he was under house arrest in Rome, chained continuously to a member of Caesar's elite Praetorian Guard (see Philippians 1:12-14).

Paul states that contentment transcends every changing external circumstance. Note Paul's language throughout Philippians 4:4-13: "Rejoice in the Lord *always*. I will say it again: Rejoice!" (v. 4). "Do not be anxious about *anything,* but *in* [not *for*] *everything,* by prayer and petition, *with thanksgiving* [thank God in whatever circumstance you find yourself], present your requests to God" (v. 6). "I have learned to be content *whatever the circumstances*. I know what it is to be in need, and I know what it is to have plenty. I have learned the secret of being content *in any and every situation*, whether *well fed or hungry,* whether living *in plenty* or *in want*. I can do *everything* through him who gives me strength" (vv. 11-13).

Paul appears to be on to something that we just don't quite comprehend. His mindset is out of step with the way most of us view life. Somehow he learned the secret of contentment in all the variables of life; his spirit found an anchor that refused to be unmoored in the midst of the churning seas or even the calm waters.

1. Paul knew that there are no barriers to God's love. He understood that you cannot erect a prison wall high enough to keep the love of God out. It is a reality applied directly to the human heart in the presence of the Holy Spirit poured out on us by our Father: "And hope does not disappoint us, because God has poured out his love into our hearts by the Holy Spirit, whom he has given us" (Romans 5:5).

The Holy Spirit is none other than the Spirit of Jesus who comes to live in our hearts. What makes someone a Christian? Quite simply a Christian is one who has received the indwelling presence of Jesus through the Holy Spirit. A Christian is one who is *in Christ,* and who has *Christ in* them. Jesus promised that upon his leaving this earth he would send a replacement who could take up residence inside of us: "And I will ask the Father, and he will give you another Counselor to be with you forever—the Spirit of truth. . . . For he lives with you and will be *in you.* I will not leave you as orphans [fatherless]; *I will come to you*" (John 14:16-18). I believe that our greatest fear is that we will be abandoned in our time of need. Jesus addressed that fear when he said, "I am with you always, to the very end of the age" (Matthew 28:20).

This is the love that embraced Paul's heart even as he was confined against his will in a Roman jail. James K. Baxter put it this way: "Lovers have many ways of expressing their love, but especially two. One is the words, 'I love you.' The other is the kiss. God's word to me, reduced to essence, is 'I love you.' His Spirit, as the mystics long ago observed, is his kiss."[1] To receive the Spirit is to allow ourselves to be kissed.

Difficult circumstances are the test of faith. If our faith doesn't hold up when life is in the pits, what good is it? One of the favorite hymns of the church came from the pen of a Chicago businessman by the name of Horatio Spafford. After losing everything in the Great Chicago Fire of 1871, he rebuilt his business and became rather prosperous. He then came to the conclusion that he wanted to serve Christ without distraction and therefore decided to move his entire family to Jerusalem. Because of some unfinished business, he put his wife and four daughters on a ship in New York, sailing for France, with the promise that he would join them shortly. However, while their ship was in transit, it was rammed by another ship and sank. He received a two-word telegram from his wife that simply read, "Saved Alone." His four daughters had been lost at sea.

Spafford booked passage on a liner to join his wife. While on the trip, he was shown the very spot where the ship carrying his wife and daughters had gone down. It was then that he wrote the hymn "It Is Well with My Soul." The first verse reads,

When peace, like a river, attendeth
    my way,
When sorrows like sea billows roll;
Whatever my lot, Thou has taught
    me to say,
It is well, it is well with my soul.

Like Paul, Spafford found a safe place in the heart of God that was an inner fortress of contentment.

2. Paul knew that we are the favored, graced children of God. This is the message that the Holy Spirit speaks to our hearts and which governs our perspective. It is the same message that the Father spoke to the heart of his Son. The Father is crazy about us.

When Jesus began his public ministry, he presented himself to John for baptism. As Jesus was coming out of the water, the Holy Spirit descended in the form of a dove, and the voice of the Father spoke a message of encouragement. In Mark's version, the Father speaks directly to the Son: *"You* are my Son, chosen and marked by my love, pride of my life" (1:11 *The Message*). The Father wants the Son to know the place he has in his heart. In Matthew's version, the Father speaks to the crowd like a proud papa: *"This* is my Son, chosen and marked by my love, delight of my life" (3:17 *The Message*). It is as if the Father cannot contain himself—"You know who this is. . . . This is my Son. . . . My buttons are busting!"

If you are a parent you know how the Father is feeling. My daughter graduated from medical school in May of 2002. I warned her ahead of time that I intended to make an absolute fool of myself and her. When her name was called to receive her hood, I rose to my feet and shouted as loud as much as my lungs could exhale, "Way to go, Aimee!" (As I like to say, I had paid a lot of money for that privilege.)

Of all the things the Father could have said to the Son at the beginning of his ministry, why these words? The Father knew where the Son's life was headed. It would end on a cross. There would be no greater challenge and no moment that would produce more doubt than when Jesus would fall before the Father in the garden of Gethsemane and cry to his Daddy, "Abba, Father, let this cup pass from me." Jesus was essentially saying, "If there is any other way besides going to the cross, make it happen." He could have said, "If you love me . . . you wouldn't allow this to happen." Yet Jesus didn't say that. Even the cross was an expression of the Father's love—for us. What the Son needed to know at the beginning of his ministry as the central foundational truth was the special place he had in the Father's heart, because there would be circumstances that could call that into question.

Paul experienced a similar message of the heart that transcended his circumstances. He never complained about his rotten circumstances as if they were contrary to God's love for him because he knew that those of us in Christ have, in a sense, the same standing before God as Jesus did. What is the message that the Holy Spirit speaks to our hearts according to Paul? "And by him we cry, 'Abba, Father.' The Spirit himself testifies with our spirit that we are God's children" (Romans 8:15-16). To have the Holy Spirit—the spirit of Jesus—in us is to also be placed under the special favor of God. In Christ, we are viewed as his beloved. What the Father says to the Son he says to us: "You are my child, chosen and marked by my love, pride of my life."

3. Paul knew that the love of God through the Holy Spirit is the spirit of the Christian community. It's not just a privatized, individualistic experience. Rarely, if ever, is the Holy Spirit biblically considered the possession of a person; rather, he's revealed as the one who indwells a people called the church or the body of Christ.

Where else do we encounter the love of God beyond the message of the heart? God's love comes through his people. The church as the body of Christ is nothing less than the heart of Jesus lived out in the presence of one another.

We can face almost anything in life if we are loved through it by God's people. That is the gift we give to each other. A friend and teaching partner shared the following story about the healing power of the Christian community. A young couple lost their daughter suddenly because of a common virus that began raging through her body. After her daughter had passed away, the mother wrote, "In a short span of three days, she went from a happy, active child sitting next to me at dinner to a little girl whose brain could no longer function due to spontaneous bleeding."

Losing their daughter in such a dramatically rapid fashion raised all the inevitable "why" questions. In a letter recounting the tragedy, the mother addressed the common futility experienced in the face of senseless loss: "Why live a 'good' life if bad things will still happen?" Yet she went on to say, "Quite frankly we have found the answer to be an easy one—because good people have good family and friends to get them through those bad times. . . . All you good people have been pivotal in getting us through this terrible time in our lives." She wrote this in the context of the Christian community.

Paul describes the rhythm of relationships in the body of Christ. "If one part suffers," he says, "every part suffers with it; if one part is honored, every part rejoices with it" (1 Corinthians 12:26). Love does not necessarily change the difficult circumstances, but to be loved through them makes it bearable.

I recall with great pleasure a moment when I was on the receiving end of the faith community's loving support. Following cancer surgery, I needed a series of thirty-seven radiation treatments. I was not shy in soliciting the prayers of the faithful. As I lay stretched out on the radiation table for my first treatment with the beam ready to be focused on the appropriate spot, I was told to lie perfectly still for the eight minutes it would take to complete the machine's rotation. In the stillness of the moment I began to visualize the Christian community upholding me in prayer. My emotions were hijacked by my internal response. I became giddy with joy over the thought of being surrounded in love by the people of God. I actually had to dampen my joy because it made my body start to gyrate in ways that would compromise the radiation treatment. The presence of Christ in the people of God can carry us so that we experience this kind of love and joy.

The secret to Paul's contentment was that he was able to accept the circumstances of life as they were; he was able to tell the Philippians, "Do not be anxious about anything, but in everything, by prayer and petition, *with thanksgiving,* present your requests to God" (Philippians 4:6). By adding "with thanksgiving," Paul was saying that there are no circumstances through which God cannot work to bring about his good.

When Catherine Marshall, author and wife of well-known preacher Peter Marshall, was wrestling with an extended bout of tuberculosis, she discovered a very important distinction. There is a huge difference between resignation and relinquishment. Accepting our circumstances does not mean adopting an attitude of resignation or Christian fatalism. The Scripture does not say to thank God "for" everything, but "in" everything. The late pastor John Claypool notes that when he lost his ten-year-old daughter to leukemia, much of what was intended by others to be consoling advice was nothing more than fatalism: "We must not question God; we must not try to understand. We have no right to ask or inquire into the ways of God with

people. The way out is to submit. We must silently and totally surrender. We must accept what God does without a word or a murmur." The implication: It was God's intention that his daughter die. Resign. And, as Marshall writes, "Resignation lies down quietly in the dust of the universe from which God seems to have fled, and the door of Hope swings shut."[2]

On the contrary, the Scripture does not teach that we are pawns to some impersonal force which cannot be changed but rather emphasizes that we are in relationship with a loving Father who is good and who has our best interest at heart. Understanding this is what moves us from resignation to relinquishment. Throughout Marshall's eighteen-month period confined to her bed with tuberculosis she pleaded with God to change her circumstance. In fact, she attempted to manipulate God to get the outcome she wanted—healing. She bargained with him, telling him that if he healed her, then she would serve him. She wrote letters of contrition to people she had wronged in any way, thinking the illness was somehow a judgment of God on her. Finally, though, she got to the point where she was able to say to God, "Lord, I'm beaten, finished. God, you decide what you want for me the rest of my life. I've discovered I want you more than my health." Once she relinquished her life and circumstances to God, along with her demanding spirit that things be different, a slow physical healing began to occur.

The prayer of relinquishment is rooted in the belief that we have a personal relationship with a loving God who can be trusted to bring good out of any circumstance of life. We must remember that Paul wrote Philippians from prison. He could have had an argument with God, asking, "Why did you allow this to happen to me? First of all, these accommodations are substandard and not befitting an apostle. Second, I need to be out following up on those churches I've started. How can it be a good thing that I'm confined to this hole? And third, Lord, there are new territories out there to conquer. What is wrong with you? Is this any way to run a kingdom?" Yet Paul's perspective was that God always opens up his possibilities regardless of the circumstances.

I have a treasure that I keep in my files. It is a letter written to me by my mother during a period of intense anxiety and anguish over my future. Observing my pain she wrote, "There is a special bond between parent and child. When the child hurts, the parent hurts. We want the very best for our children, but we must also trust God for what is best." She was essentially saying, *I don't merely want you to be happy; I want only what God wants for you.* She continued, "First, God's time is not our time. We are asked to wait and pray and trust. If we humble ourselves before God and do not let pride get in the way, through it all we have God's great

peace. It truly is a peace that passes all understanding. I felt it when I went into surgery 4 years ago [for breast cancer], and I have called upon Him many times when fear welled up in my heart with a pain that I thought might be the return of the cancer. He has never failed me." "Never" is underlined.

Paul has let us in on his secret. He discovered the secret of a life of contentment, joy and peace, which transcends the roller-coaster circumstances of life. It is a life rooted in the ever-present love of God through the Holy Spirit within us and the Christian community. There are no barriers that can be erected against this love. Paul triumphantly concludes the eighth chapter of Romans—where he has already asserted that God works all things together for good—with this crescendo: "For I am convinced that neither death nor life, neither angels nor demons, neither the present nor the future, nor any powers, neither height nor depth, nor anything else in all creation, will be able to separate us from the love of God that is in Christ Jesus our Lord" (Romans 8:38-39).

Paul's lens through which he viewed life is our window into a transformed mind. If we are to love God with all of our mind, it begins by aligning our sight with the way Paul viewed this life and the life to come.

---

[1]James K. Baxter, quoted in David Watson, *Called and Committed: World-Changing Discipleship* (Wheaton, Ill.: Harold Shaw, 2000), p. 80.
[2]Catherine Marshall, *Beyond Our Selves* (New York: McGraw-Hill, 1961), p. 94.

Reading Study Guide

1. How would you describe the transformation that is needed as we grow up in Christ?

   What role does the mind play in this transformation?

2. Paul is on to something that most of us don't seem to get. What is it that Paul seems to grasp that we often have a hard time comprehending?

3. Do you agree or disagree that Paul's contentment in whatever present circumstances he was in and his future hope are so rare as to be almost unique? Why?

4. The reading mentions three reasons for Paul's mindset. Summarize each:

   a. There are no barriers to the presence of Christ's love:

   b. We are the beloved and favored children of the Father:

   c. We experience the love of God through his people:

5. How do these truths affect the perspective you have on your life?

6. Catherine Marshall discovered the difference between resignation and relinquishment. What is that difference?

7. What do we have to believe in order to relinquish ourselves to God?

   How might relinquishment to God's love be tested with a specific circumstance in your life right now?

8. Summarize the mind of Christ that Paul displays in his outlook.

Going Deeper

Catherine Marshall. *Beyond Our Selves*. New York: McGraw-Hill, 1961. Marshall tells her own faith story in this work, sharing her discovery of the difference between resignation and relinquishment and the implications of each approach for our understanding of the nature of God.

7 / The Transformation of the Mind

LOOKING AHEAD

MEMORY VERSE: Philippians 4:8
BIBLE STUDY: Psalm 19
READING: The Power of the Mind

 Core Truth

Why is the mind the primary location of our transformation into Christlikeness?

The mind is the most powerful faculty in the human makeup. The ideas and images that shape our mind determine how we feel, how we behave and what we ultimately live for. We have been given minds so that we can search out the highest and most important truth, which is to be known and claimed by God and then to live accordingly. In Christ, we enter into a lifelong process of transformation in which we're continuously adjusting our thinking by banishing distortions of God's reality while putting on his new way of seeing.

1. Identify key words or phrases in the question and answer above, and state their meaning in your own words.

2. Restate the core truth in your own words.

3. What questions or issues does the core truth raise for you?

Memory Verse Study Guide

The quality of our life is directly related to the health of our thoughts. The apostle Paul believes that we can train our minds to think about those things that will lift our spirit and ennoble us. We need not be victims of our feelings or of the stimulants around us; we can actually choose the climate of our life by what we think. This is Paul's admonition in our memory verse.

1. *Putting it in context:* Read Philippians 4:4-13. In this broader setting Paul suggests a number of noble choices as to where we can focus our thoughts. What are they?

2. The memory verse is *Philippians 4:8*. Copy the verse verbatim.

3. In verse 8, specifically, Paul piles up a number of words to describe where our thoughts should dwell. List each of the words and give one illustration of that characteristic (e.g., true: God is light and in him is no darkness at all).

4. Paul is conversely implying that we should not place our thoughts on things that would be degrading or things that will not bring the best out of us. What might be some of the things we should avoid?

   What implications does this have for the images we dwell on (e.g., TV, movies, music, etc.) or the kind of material we read?

5. What is one specific choice you could make to jettison something that is degrading and replace it with something that is God-honoring?

✒ Inductive Bible Study Guide

"The single most important thing in our minds is our idea of God and the associated images," writes Dallas Willard.[1] So when it comes to training our thinking, the Scriptures lead us to a celebration of who God is and the wisdom that is revealed through his nature and character. Psalm 19 is the culmination of David's meditation on the Creator God and the timeless truth derived from his being. Worship is the natural outcome of an uplifted mind.

1. *Read Psalm 19.* After reading this psalm through in a couple of different translations, write down the emotions that David's words have evoked in you.

2. In verses 1-6 David views the creation as an expression of the glory of God. What images does David use to capture the connection between God's glory and creation?

3. In verses 7-9 what descriptive word is used in each verse to capture the goodness that is derived from God's law?

   What value would you ascribe to each of these words?

4. What images does David use in verses 10-11 to convey the value of following God's law?

What do these images motivate you to change in your life?

5. What, then, does David's contemplation of the value of the law lead to (vv. 12-13)?

6. What advice does David have for himself?

7. How does verse 14 apply to some specific area of your life or relationships?

8. How does David view God at the very end of the psalm (v. 14)?

If how we think about God is the most important thing about us, it's important for us to know how we're actually thinking about him! What images do you think form your understanding of God?

9. What new understanding of God do you have from the images David uses in Psalm 19?

Reading: The Power of the Mind

In the previous chapter we looked at the apostle Paul and his belief that transformation is located in the mind; he understood that the mind—not our eyes—is the vehicle through which we see life. Jesus affirmed this when he explained that our minds provide the light to our bodies: "The eye is the lamp of the body. If your eyes are good, your whole body will be full of light. But if your eyes are bad, your whole body will be full of darkness. If then the light within you is darkness, how great is that darkness!" (Matthew 6:22-23). What allows us to see clearly so that our body is full of light? The state of our minds.

Paul served as our model of someone who had a transformed mind, and he calls us to "be transformed by the renewing of [our] mind" as well. We observed that Paul seemed to be in on a secret about how to view life with a refreshed outlook that was rooted in the implications of the decisive events of the death and resurrection of Jesus. He knew that the secret to contentment in this life was the abiding presence of the love of Jesus Christ, which would only be intensified when he met him face to face. Paul, therefore, could sit in prison and proclaim that he had learned to be content in any and every situation.

In this chapter we want to make this all very practical. The mind is the filter through which the light passes that allows us to see clearly or dimly. If the filter has accumulated junk then our seeing will be distorted, but if it's clean we will see clearly. Figure one provides a model of how we see with our minds and then respond (with anger, for example, or with any number of other emotions).

Have you ever said to someone, "You made me angry"? Is that a true statement? Can someone make you angry? We might, of course, have a legitimate right to be angry—if someone has betrayed us, for example. But in fact, anger is a result of

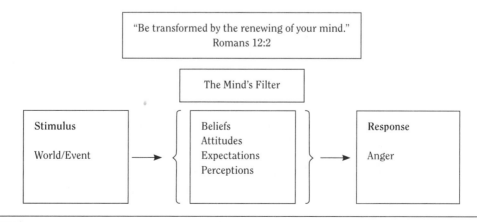

Figure 1.

the meaning we give to a stimulus. As figure one illustrates, the stimulus must pass through the filter of our belief system, which is what makes up the content of our mind. Our response happens so rapidly we don't even see the process; we're not aware of the filter through which the stimulus has passed to create the response. But our emotional responses really are a byproduct of a thought that has gone through the filter of our minds. Therefore, to say, "You made me angry," is generally not a factual statement. Ultimately, our goal is to have a mind—a filter or belief system—that actually produces the fruit of the spirit. More about that in a moment.

THE MAKEUP OF THE MIND

First we have to look at five elements that make up the content or filter of our mind: beliefs, attitudes, expectations, perceptions and the spirit of the mind. These serve as the grid through which we see life. So the renewal of our minds must be focused on the content of these five elements. They need to be brought into conformity to the truth about God and life as revealed in Scripture.

Let's take a look at these so that we can see what makes up our mental maps.

Beliefs. Our minds contain beliefs. There is the old scientific adage, "Seeing is believing." What we may not be aware of, though, is that the reverse is true: "Believing is seeing." We see what we believe. The classic illustration of this is the story of the ship RMS *Titanic*. It was the belief that the ship was unsinkable that led to its de-

mise. It did, after all, have a double bottom, and sixteen watertight compartments. Though RMS *Titanic* received several warnings over a two-day period that it was in iceberg-infested waters, there was, apparently, no need to heed these warnings because the ship was considered impregnable. Even the slow response to abandoning ship once it had been hit was based on the belief that the ship could not go down. They saw what they believed.

Our beliefs are what cause us to interpret what we see in particular ways. For example, imagine walking down the streets of any major city. You come across a homeless person wrapped in a blanket and huddled in the doorway of an office building, a cup in their hand extended for help. Your reaction will depend on what you believe. If you have the belief that every person on the streets is an able-bodied individual who should get a job, your attitude may be one of disdain and disgust. But, on the other hand, if you believe that God has a special heart for the dispossessed, you'll see the person differently. You may have internalized the Scripture that teaches us that Jesus comes disguised in the form of the poor and the disadvantaged; "as you have done it unto the least of these," Jesus said, "you have done it unto me." If this is what you believe, you'll likely respond with compassion and care. The challenge is to bring our belief system into accord with biblical values.

Irrational beliefs. One of the ways our seeing is distorted is through irrational beliefs. These are "truths" that take up space in our mind that have zero evidence to support them and that are impossible to live up to.

You can usually recognize these irrational beliefs by the words that tend to come before them: "I've got to," "I must" or "I ought to." The "shoulds" and "oughts" serve as absolutes and therefore stand in judgment over us.

Psychologist Albert Ellis identified a number of these irrational beliefs.[2]

- I must be loved and liked by everyone.

- I must be loved at all times, without exception.

- I must be competent in all that I do.

- I must never fail.

- I have no control over my happiness.

- Everything bad that happens to me is a catastrophe.

- I must have everyone's approval.

- I must not let other people down.

Can you relate to any of these? Would you add your own? One of my irrational beliefs that haunts me is a combination of a few from Ellis's list: "I must be competent in all that I undertake and never fail in anything I do." Even while writing this chapter I was wondering if it would come together. I could feel myself questioning my value and worth. I do that same kind of questioning in my work. For example, some Sunday mornings someone comes through "the greeting line" after a service I've preached in and says, "You know, you're getting better." I wonder to myself,

How am I supposed to take that? I think it's meant as a compliment, but my first thought is, *Better compared to what? Better than the lousy preacher I used to be?* I allow a statement like that to take up space in my spirit because I believe that my worth is dependent on being competent in all I do.

Transformation, in part, means identifying and replacing these irrational beliefs with God-centered ones, like "In Christ I am a beloved child of God. My value has an unshakable foundation."

The "you ares" that become the "I ams." In addition to these irrational beliefs, many of us have beliefs about ourselves that are lingering messages from our childhood years. As Dr. David Seamands explains it, the "you ares" of childhood can become the "I ams" of adulthood.[3] Some of you, for example, may have repeatedly heard statements like, "If there is a wrong way to do things, you'll find it"; "Why can't you be more like your brother or sister?"; "You were trouble before you were born"; or "No wonder you don't have any friends."

Author and pastor David Seamands recounts the story of Barry, a man who grew up in a home where he heard his father regularly say, "You're a bum. You'll always be a bum." On the day of his college graduation—an event his father did not attend—Barry heard these same words from his father again. This became one of the dominant narratives of his adult years. After losing an important position with a major insurance company, he entered counseling. Though Barry was intelligent and an eloquent speaker—some would say even charismatic—within a year of starting a new job he would find a way to self-destruct. His father's "you are" had become Barry's "I am"; his mind had become wrapped in a cocoon of insecurity and self-loathing. Barry needed to be reparented by the Father who loved him so much that he was worth the price of the Father's Son. Likewise, we too need to identify the "I ams" that form a negative narrative in our life and replace them with our Lord's affirmative perspective about us.

Attitudes. Another aspect of our minds is our attitudes. Attitudes are predispositions. If you mention my grandchildren, I am predisposed to smile and take on an attitude of warmth. But on the other hand, there are things and people that I am predisposed to respond to negatively. We have people in our lives of whom we have not formed a flattering point of view; hearing them mentioned or seeing them behave in a certain way only reinforces our predisposed attitude. The only way to have our feelings change is to first consciously change how we view the person or situation. For example, I know a man who consistently disrupts classes he's in. His presence used to evoke anger in me. But then I decided to get to know him in other circumstances, and once I did so I found out I really liked him. Charles Swindoll, a nationally known Bible teacher and communicator, has written, "The longer I live, the more I realize the impact of attitude on life. . . . The remarkable thing is we have a choice every day regarding the attitude we

will embrace that day. . . . We cannot change the past. We cannot change the fact that people will act in a certain way. . . . I am convinced that life is 10% what happens to me and 90% how I react to it. We are in charge of our attitudes."[4]

Expectations. Then there are expectations. There is nothing more disappointing than false expectations, which we hold on to contrary to all the evidence. What is the popular definition of insanity? "Doing the same thing over and over again and expecting different results." We do this with the people and situations in our life; they do the same things over and over again, and we set ourselves up for disappointment or hurt by expecting them to act differently. If we accept that some people are the way they are, instead of expecting them to be different, we will free ourselves from frustration and disappointment.

There is a story about a woman whose husband didn't make her feel very special. He never did the little things that express affection. When new neighbors moved in across the street, the woman started peeking through the curtains to observe the husband and wife. She couldn't help but notice that, every night when he got home from work, he would bring flowers or a little gift to his wife, and she would run to meet him at the front door for a hug and a kiss. After watching this for weeks she decided to drop a not-so-subtle hint to her husband. One night, the moment her husband walked in the door, she hit him with it. "Have you noticed we have new neighbors across the street?" she asked.

As he dropped his briefcase and fell into his easy chair in front of the television he replied, "Yeah, I've noticed we have new neighbors."

She continued, "But have you noticed what they do every night?"

"No, dear, I haven't noticed."

"Every night when he comes home, he gives her a big kiss, he hugs her, and he almost always brings her a special gift. How come you never do that?"

Her husband stared at her with a puzzled look on his face and said, "Honey, I can't do that. I hardly know the woman."[5]

The woman drove herself crazy expecting affection from a man who did not know how to give it. Every night she was disappointed because of her expectation that, if her husband loved her, he would show it in a certain way. Adjusting our expectations to reality will relieve us of much disappointment.

Perceptions. The fourth element that forms the filter of our mind is perception. Perceptions are usually judgments we've made based on minimal data. The aforementioned Chuck Swindoll tells a not-so-flattering story that illustrates this well. One summer he was speaking at a week-long Bible conference. The first night a couple introduced themselves to him in a friendly fashion; they seemed especially glad to be there. But Swindoll noticed as the week went on that the man fell asleep at every one of the meetings. By midweek he recognized feelings of irritation rising inside him; within the first ten minutes of his speaking this guy was out like a light.

By Friday evening Swindoll had concluded that the man must be there under duress. It must have been his wife's idea to come, and this man must be some kind of spiritual pygmy. After the Friday evening session, the woman asked for a few moments of Swindoll's time. He was expecting her to share her unhappiness about living with a man who had little interest in spiritual things. Instead, she informed him that it was her husband's final wish to be at this conference. "You see," she said, "you are his favorite Bible teacher. He has only a few weeks to live. He is on such a heavy dose of medication that it makes him sleepy." Swindoll was stunned and felt deeply rebuked for the judgment he had made about this brother.[6]

Swindoll's story leads us to self-examination. We are constantly making judgments without all the facts. Whether it be an ethnic stereotype or a prejudice of whatever kind, we are sizing up others on the basis of superficial data. Ask God to help you monitor your perceptions in order to see when it is you are prone to instant assessments.

The spirit of our minds. The last element is the spirit of our minds. We see through our minds, and our minds create the climate or tone out of which we lead our lives. In Ephesians 4:23 Paul adds another nuance to the transformation of our minds. He tells us, "Be made new in the attitude [or spirit] of your minds." What is the spirit or attitude of the mind? It is the inner atmosphere in which we exist. Archibald Hart, a Christian psychologist, calls this our self-talk. It is so second-nature to us that we may not even recognize it. Yet at all times we carry on inner conversation or dialogue. For example, since the beginning of this reading you have been processing it within yourself. For some of you, this may have caused you to note something important you want to remember. Others of you may be thinking to yourself, *This guy's all wet.* Still others of you have checked out and are thinking about something else. But you're all talking to yourself silently.

This means that the way to get in touch with what needs to change in your mind is by listening to yourself. There it is again—self-awareness and listening as a path by which we grow. Many of the same practices that I encouraged you to engage in as listening posts in chapter three are the very things that will lead you to the renewal of your mind.

The mind, then, is the filter through which we see, and it is made up of beliefs, attitudes, expectations, perceptions and spirit. This just demonstrates the complexity of what goes into our seeing.

THE WAY OF TRANSFORMATION

With those elements in view, there are two inviolable laws we also need to be aware of, as they greatly influence the transformation of the mind. The first is the *law of cognition:* we are what we think. The King James Version of Proverbs 23:7 says, "As [a man] thinketh, . . . so is he." Similarly, James Allen, in his little book *As a Man Thinketh,* writes, "The body is the servant of the mind. It obeys the operations of the mind, whether they be deliberately chosen or automatically expressed. At the bidding of unlawful thoughts the body sinks rapidly into disease and decay; at the command of glad and beautiful thoughts it becomes clothed with youthfulness and beauty."[7] The quality or tone of our life is largely impacted by where we rest our minds. John Ortberg puts it this way: "The way you think creates your attitudes; the way you think shapes your emotions; the way you think governs your behavior; the way you think deeply influences your immune system and vulnerability to illness. Everything about you flows out of the way you think."[8]

There is no more dramatic statement about the power of the mind than from the pen of Victor Frankl in *Man's Search for Meaning.* Frankl was a Holocaust survivor who reflected on those who remained hopeful even under the horrendous conditions versus those who gave up hope. Frankl's thesis is that there is always one last vestige of freedom even under intolerable circumstances: it is the freedom of choice with how you view your circumstances. No one can take away the attitude that you choose. Frankl writes,

> We who lived in concentration camps can remember the men who walked through the huts comforting others, giving away their last piece of bread. They may have been few in number, but they offer sufficient proof that everything can be taken from a man

but one thing: the last of human freedoms—to choose one's attitude in any given set of circumstances.

And there were always choices to make. Every day, every hour, offered the opportunity to make a decision, a decision which determined whether you would or would not submit to those powers which threatened to rob you of your very self, your inner freedom.[9]

The good news about the law of cognition, as Frankl reminds us, is that we can choose the way we think—which means we can change the way we think. And changing the way we think can lead to an entirely different quality of life. But how do we change our thinking? That's where the second law comes in: the *law of exposure*.[10] This is Paul's point in Philippians 4:8 when he says, "Summing it all up, friends, I'd say you'll do best by filling your minds and meditating on things true, noble, reputable, authentic, compelling, gracious—the best, not the worst; the beautiful, not the ugly; things to praise, not things to curse" *(The Message)*. Paul asserts that our minds will think about what we expose them to. We can't continue to absorb fearful pictures of the future, sensual images that promise fulfillment, hateful speech that runs down others, without being impacted by it. As John Ortberg observes, "The events we attend, the material we read, the music we hear, the images we watch, the conversations we hold, the daydreams we dwell on, all shape our mind."[11] This leads us back to Paul's admonition from Philippians 4:8 to lift our sights to higher things.

Can you see that it is the mind that regulates the thermostat of our bodies? The mind is the quality-control gate for our feelings. All feelings have a precipitating thought. Dallas Willard puts it this way: "Our thoughts are the most basic sources of life. They determine our orientation toward everything we do and evoke the feelings that frame our world and motivate our actions. Our power over thoughts is of great and indispensable assistance in directing and controlling our feelings."[12]

Because ideas and images are the primary way Satan attempts to defeat God's work in the world and in our lives, and because our emotions and vision stem directly from our minds, we must pay careful attention to what makes up the filter of our mind. The law of exposure tells us to continuously clean our filter by taking on the perspective that Scripture provides. A seminary professor of mine used to say repeatedly that we study and absorb ourselves in Scripture and the spiritual disciplines in order to "think God's thoughts after him."[13] Right thinking will lead to right living and feeling.

I love the *Peanuts* cartoon where Linus and Lucy are involved in substantive dialogue. Lucy is worried over the volume of rain. It has been raining for so long that she wonders whether there will be another worldwide flood as in Noah's day. Linus informs her that it won't happen. Referring to Genesis 9, Linus reminds Lucy that God promised never to flood the earth again. Lucy says, "Well, that takes a load off my mind." While sucking on his blanket, Linus replies, "Yes, sound theology does that."

Ultimately our minds must be formed around the reality of what God is actually like and who we are in light of this truth. Our life is to be lived in the light of the death and resurrection of Jesus. We know that through these events God was willing to pay the ultimate price to buy our life back and that he has opened the doorway to an eternal future by his defeat of death through the resurrection. We saw in our last chapter that Paul took on a new mind because he lived inside of these truths. Nothing could separate him from the love of God. He was God's beloved child whose future was secure.

Again, Dallas Willard says it well, "The gospel of Jesus directly repudiates all false information about God and, therewith, about the meaning of human life; and it works to undermine the power of those ideas and images that structure life away from God. But for it to have this effect we must *use* our ability to think."[14] The difference between darkness and light is where we place our thoughts and the assumption upon which we build our life.

I must close with this humorous story of a woman who had a transformed mind. This woman was meeting with her pastor to plan her funeral service. After they had selected the music, the Scriptures and the rest of the details, she said to her pastor, "One more thing."

"What's that?" replied the pastor.

"I want to be buried with a fork in my right hand."

The pastor had to admit that in all of his years this was probably the most unusual request he'd received. She explained, "In all my years going to church functions, whenever food was involved, my favorite part was when whoever was cleaning up the dishes of the main course would lean over and say, 'You can keep your fork.' It was my favorite part because I knew something great was coming. It wasn't JELL-O. It was something of substance—cake or pie.

"So I just want people to see me later there in my casket with a fork in my right hand, and I want them to wonder, what's with the fork? Then I want you to tell them: 'Something better is coming. Keep your fork.'" This woman had taken on Paul's viewpoint that "the best was yet to come."

---

[1]Dallas Willard, *Renovation of the Heart* (Colorado Springs: NavPress, 2002), p. 100.

[2]Albert Ellis, referenced in Archibald Hart, *Feeling Free* (Old Tappan, N.J.: Revell, 1979), p. 49.

[3]David Seamands, *Healing Grace: Let God Free You from the Performance Trap* (Wheaton, Ill.: Victor Books, 1988), pp. 152-53.

[4]John Maxwell, *Developing the Leader Within You* (Nashville: Thomas Nelson, 1993), p. 93.

[5]Gary Smalley with John Trent, *Love Is a Decision* (Dallas: Word, 1989), p. 16.

[6]Charles Swindoll, *The Grace Awakening* (Dallas: Word, 1990), p. 165.

[7]James Allen, quoted in Hart, *Feeling Free*, p. 43.

[8]John Ortberg, *If You Want to Walk on Water, You've Got to Get Out of the Boat* (Grand Rapids: Zondervan, 2001), p. 162.

[9]Victor Frankl, *Man's Search for Meaning* (New York: Washington Square Press, 1959), p. 104.
[10]Ortberg, *If You Want to Walk on Water,* p. 162.
[11]Ibid., p. 163.
[12]Willard, *Renovation of the Heart,* p. 96.
[13]Dr. Daniel Fuller, Fuller Theological Seminary professor of hermeneutics. An often-heard statement while I was a student of Dr. Fuller between 1968-1973.
[14]Willard, *Renovation of the Heart,* p. 104.

Reading Study Guide

1. How would you characterize the power of the mind?

2. What is it that makes up the mind?

   How does the mind serve as a filter through which our eyes see?

3. Describe each element of the filter of our mind:
   Beliefs:

   Attitudes:

   Expectations:

   Perceptions:

   The spirit of our minds:

4. Identify a personal "irrational belief" that negatively impacts the quality of your thinking. What truth from God would you put in its place?

5. Can you recognize any destructive "you ares" of childhood that have become the "I ams" of adulthood? Explain your self-perception.

6. Evaluate the quality of what you expose your mind to. How have those elements shaped your worldview?

   What changes do you need to make?

7. If the Scripture is the primary place we "think God's thoughts after him," what place does reading and meditating on God's Word have in your life? Choose from the options below:
   - I read and meditate daily on a portion of God's Word.
   - I read and meditate several times a week on God's Word.
   - I find myself searching the Scriptures to look for answers to life challenges.
   - I attempt to base my thoughts and opinions on a biblical perspective.
   - I have a sporadic approach to reading and reflecting on God's Word.
   - I have a hard time relating to the content of the Bible and making sense of it.
   - I desire to have a greater hunger for his Word than I currently do.
   - Other: _____

   Explain why you picked the option you did.

Going Deeper

Willard, Dallas. *Renovation of the Heart.* Colorado Springs: NavPress, 2002. Willard's discussion of the power and place of the mind in the process of transformation (chapters
six and seven) in this modern classic makes it clear why Paul saw the mind as the primary place of renewal. Willard shows that it's the mind that has the freedom to bring
the heart and body into alignment with the commands of God.

Part Four

LOVE THE LORD YOUR GOD . . .
WITH ALL YOUR STRENGTH

Perhaps the least considered and understood of all the elements of our love for God is what it means to love God with our *strength*. Because it is the least considered and understood, it is also the least appreciated. We have not grasped the importance of this element.

If strength has to do fundamentally with energy that comes from our bodily nature, then it is easy to see why we haven't focused on it. As we will explore in these next two chapters, our Christian doctrine and mindset have been invaded with a Greek dualistic framework whereby we tend to separate the body from the spirit, believing we can be spiritual with little attention to the body. Our focus has been on the inner life: feed the soul and the body will take care of itself. In chapter nine, specifically, we will counter the Greek elevation of the soul over the body and reveal it as the pagan infiltration into the Christian consciousness that it is. In both chapters eight and nine, though, we will embrace the body, in both its physical and spiritual vitality, as essential to learning to love God with all aspects of our being.

The key word in chapter eight is *discipline*. We carry in our bodies God-pleasing and God-displeasing habits. Habits get lodged into the fabric of our being. One of the apostle Paul's images of sanctification is that of a wardrobe makeover. He tells us to, in essence, empty our closets of the old tattered garments that we put on in our former way of life and fill our closets with new attire that honors God. In other words, he describes the Christian life as a lifelong process of undressing and redressing.

To enter in to this makeover requires a *disciplined* approach. Paul was a man on a mission, ready to marshal all of his energy toward the singular focus of presenting everyone mature in Christ. Like him, we too are called to be people focused on the particular call that God has given us. This requires treating the Christian life like an athlete training for competition, a soldier under orders from his commander or a farmer laboring to bring in a harvest. Even though the Christian life is about grace received, this does not at all mean we are simply carried along without effort. In fact, Paul saw a direct connection between appreciation of grace and the effort that comes as a result of it. "But by the grace of God I am what I am," he writes, "and his grace to me was not without effect. No, I worked *harder* than all of them—yet not I, but the grace of God that was with me" (1 Corinthians 15:10).

We will therefore also consider in chapter eight the role of spiritual disciplines—

practices that bring us into the presence of God's grace. The spiritual disciplines are like sails on a sail boat. Only God can provide the wind of his Spirit to ignite the impetus for movement, but we can hoist the sails to be ready when God decides to move in and through us.

In chapter nine we then go more directly after our understanding of the body and its place in our love for God, answering the question, "How do the Scriptures explain the nature of the body?" We'll see that the body is not just a temporary mode of existence that will be cast aside at death but that it is all a part of God's design. Jesus affirmed our bodily nature by taking on human flesh fully. He did not just *seem* to be human, as an early church heresy asserted (*docetism,* from the Greek for "to appear or seem"); rather, he was the complete union of the human and the divine. There could be no greater affirmation of the value and importance of the human body than Jesus' incarnation.

With the value of the body established, then, we will look at how our bodies are integral to our personhood. Everything we are and do is as bodily people. Indeed, our bodies are the locale of our redemption. Paul uses the audacious phrase "temples of the Holy Spirit" in reference to our bodies. We are the dwelling place of God. One of the implications of this is proper health. Do we treat our bodies in a way that promotes maximum health as a sign of our reverence? A second implication, clearly emphasized by Paul, is that, as part of the makeover process, we are to present the parts of our body to God as instruments of righteousness. In other words, we are to pay attention to the messages that our bodily parts send us; those messages are often indicators of where we need to focus our attention for taking off the old attire and putting on the new.

8 / Focusing Our Energy

LOOKING AHEAD

MEMORY VERSES: Colossians 1:28-29
BIBLE STUDY: Ephesians 4:17-24
READING: Disciplining Our Spirit and Body

 Core Truth

What does it mean to love God with all of our strength?

Our strength is our capacity or ability to serve God with the passion and energy he has given us as bodily creatures in order to fulfill his call upon our lives. Like athletes training for competition, farmers preparing for a harvest or soldiers under orders (2 Timothy 2:3-6), lovers of God bring their spirit and body under self-mastery in order to align all of their efforts toward fulfilling God's purpose for their life.

1. Identify key words or phrases in the question and answer above, and state their meaning in your own words.

2. Restate the core truth in your own words.

3. What questions or issues does the core truth raise for you?

Memory Verse Study Guide

The person of Paul dominates this chapter because his teaching and life are so illustrative of the focused energy that is called for to fulfill our love for God. In our memory verses Paul sums up both the substance of his call and the passion he has to fulfill it. Like him, we each have a claim from God upon our lives, and we too are to complete it with fervor. As we look at Paul's example, let's also take our spiritual temperature in order to measure our enthusiasm level.

1. *Putting it in context:* Read Colossians 1:24-27 as a backdrop to Paul's personal mission statement. What role does Paul see himself fulfilling among the Gentiles?

2. The memory verses are *Colossians 1:28-29*. Copy the verses verbatim.

3. In verse 28, Paul gives a succinct summary of his mission. How would you characterize what it is that energizes Paul's life?

4. Compare Paul's statement of his mission with the mission Jesus gave to the entire church in Matthew 28:19-20. How has Paul personalized what Jesus commanded?

5. How do you personally react to the intensity Paul conveys here?

   Excitement: This is the intensity I live my life with. Paul is my soulmate!

   Fear: I have never felt that strongly about anything in my life.

   Envy: I wish I could feel that strongly about a purpose.

   Ambivalence: I am not sure I want to be that consumed.

   Other: _____

6. Do you agree or disagree with the statement, "Paul is an extreme example of commitment, and therefore an exception to the kind of focused energy that we should have"? Explain your answer.

7. What does Paul's example teach you about loving God with all of your strength?

Inductive Bible Study Guide

Continuing with our emphasis on Paul as our primary teacher in this chapter, we turn to one of the images he uses to describe the process of transformation that is central to the Christian's walk: the image of a *makeover*. I have chosen this text because Paul paints a picture in it of the kind of intensity with which we should approach our "vocation" of becoming Christlike. He says that we need a new wardrobe as followers of Christ—that there is a set of garments representing an old way of life that needs to be taken off and exchanged for a new set of garments consistent with life in Christ. In the passage Paul shows both the need for this change and the contrasting lifestyles of the "before and after."

1. *Read Ephesians 4:17-24*. In verses 17-18, Paul centers his critique of life apart from God around terms that relate to the thought process. What words indicate this?

2. What reason does Paul give for this errant thinking (v. 18)? Put in your own words what you think Paul means.

3. According to verse 19, what are the results of a hardened heart?

   Does Paul's description accord with what you see happening to people with hardened hearts?

4. In verses 20-24, Paul describes the startling contrast between life without Christ (the "former way of life") and life in Christ ("the new self"). Summarize that contrast.

5. What is the "old self" that is to be put off?

6. What is the "new self" that is to be put on?

7. What process does Paul say we're to follow to put off the old self and put on the new self?

8. How can you work this process into your daily life? What spiritual disciplines (practices) might you need to incorporate into your daily life in order to continuously practice this "putting off" and "putting on"?

Reading: Disciplining Our Spirit and Body

We live out our love for God as bodily creatures. As we will see even more in the next chapter, being spiritual is inclusive of our bodies. So when Jesus says we are to love God with all of our strength (the word Jesus uses here for strength, *ischuos,* can also be translated "capacity," "ability" or "power"), we really do move into the physical realm. We love God by harnessing our bodily energy with passion to serve God and our neighbor.

The apostle Paul captures this emphasis through a theme that dominates his understanding of the way that the Christian life is to be lived. My one-word summary of his focus is *discipline*. Paul piles up images of athletes in training, soldiers under command and hard-working farmers. He loves using words like *training, self-control, sober, working, labor* and *focused energy* to describe the life in Christ. For example, in 1 Corinthians 9 Paul makes a direct allusion to training for the local version of the Olympic Games. In the Corinthian context, the backdrop was most likely the Isthmian Games, where athletes were required to demonstrate that they had been training for ten months if they wanted to compete. "Do you not know that in a race all the runners run, but only one gets the prize?" Paul asks. "Run in such a way as to get the prize. Everyone who competes in the games goes into strict *training*. They do it to get a crown that will not last; but we do it to get a

crown that will last forever" (1 Corinthians 9:24-25).

I would submit that the Christian life needs to be approached in the same way that an athlete trains to compete. Practice, discipline, repetition, routine. Michael Jordan, when he was in his prime, routinely pulled out wins in the waning moments of games. How? Because he simply tried at the end of a game? No. Even though he is a very gifted athlete, he spent hours out of public sight, practicing his jump shot and free throws. He worked harder than everyone else even though he had so much natural talent.

Note Paul's "how much more" argument in verses 24 and 25. In human athletic competition a person gets accolades in the moment, but they are fading and fleeting. We, however, are after a crown that will last forever. Therefore, *how much more* should we be training to be made over into the resemblance of the One we follow?

PAUL'S PERSONAL MISSION
STATEMENT
As exhibit A, Paul puts forth his own life as one who has attempted to bring everything in his being to bear on his God-assigned role. In writing his own mission statement (which is reflective of the mission statement Jesus gave the church in Matthew 28:18-20), Paul states his call and then follows it up by describing the atti-

tude in which he carries it out: "We proclaim him [Jesus], admonishing and teaching everyone with all wisdom, so that we may present everyone perfect in Christ. *To this end I labor, struggling with all his energy, which so powerfully works in me"* (Colossians 1:28-29). Note how Paul strings together his words of passion. He *labors,* meaning it requires hard work and exertion to complete his call. He *struggles* against the lethargy and laziness that could have their hold on him. Then he speaks of the energy *(energeian)* of God energizing *(energoumenen)* him to complete his call. The word for "energy" used here is the same one Paul uses in 1 Corinthians 12 as a synonym for spiritual gifts; the NIV translates it as "working": "There are different kinds of *working [energematon],* but the same God works *[energon]* all of them in all men" (v. 6). In others words, when we are operating in our giftedness, we are energized, empowered, in the flow, living out what God has designed us to do. But this still requires discipline to stay focused. It's similar to how Dallas Willard describes grace: "Grace is opposed to *earning,* not to effort."[1]

To underscore the centrality of the discipline required to love God, Paul repeatedly uses either *self-control* or *sober* when describing the Christian life. For example, *self-control* is the last fruit of the Spirit listed in Galatians 5:22-23. The root word means to have power or lordship over all things. It is the word that the NIV translates as "training" in 1 Corinthians 9:25 —in this case, athletic training or self-

mastery, as we saw above. Athletes practice strenuously so that in competition they can respond automatically, having brought their bodies under control. Similarly, Paul tells us that a quality of those who aspire to leadership is *self-control* or being *sober.* In these instances, *sober* doesn't just refer to not being under the influence of alcohol or drugs but to having our wits about us; we are not to be under the control of an outside influence (Romans 12:3; 1 Timothy 3:2; Titus 1:8; 2:2, 5, 6, 12; 1 Peter 1:13; 4:7; 5:8).

John Stott wonderfully sums up Paul's intent: "You can become a Christian in a moment, but not a mature Christian. Christ can enter, cleanse and forgive you in a matter of seconds, but it will take much longer for your character to be transformed and molded to his will. It takes only a few minutes for a bride and bridegroom to be married, but in the rough-and-tumble of their home it may take many years for two strong wills to be dovetailed into one. So when we receive Christ, a moment of commitment will lead to a lifetime of adjustment."[2]

A TRAINING MENTALITY

We are to adopt the same attitude toward becoming like Christ as an athlete has toward training for competition, a musician toward mastering an instrument or a soldier toward preparing for battle. Becoming like Christ is our vocation or calling in life. We're to place all of our strength at the disposal of the God who gives us strength to serve him.

The process of growth. In Ephesians 4, Paul compares the process of transformation to a lifetime makeover. We are to "put off [our] old self, which is being corrupted by its deceitful desires . . . and . . . put on the new self, created to be like God in true righteousness and holiness" (Ephesians 4:22, 24). In other words, take off the old, tattered, smelly garments that represent your pre-Christian life and put on a whole new set of clothing that is befitting a follower of Christ. We probably have all seen the makeover shows where a spouse complains that their partner dresses in a slovenly way around the house, and they want to see this person made over into the beautiful or handsome person they can be. So the person nominated prances onto the stage looking like a slob, but at the end of the program, they emerge transformed. The studio audience oohs and aahs at the unveiling of this "new" person.

A story about an Amish boy and his father also illustrates this idea of old and new. One day the two of them found themselves in a modern shopping mall. They were amazed at everything but especially the two shiny, silver walls that would move apart and slide back together again. The boy asked, "What is this, Father?" The father, never having seen an elevator, said he had no idea. While the boy and his father were watching with amazement, an older woman in a wheelchair rolled up to the moving walls and pressed the button. When the walls opened she wheeled herself between them into a small room. The walls closed behind her. The boy and his

father watched the numbers above the walls light up sequentially and then reverse as they came back down. Finally the walls opened up again and a gorgeous young blond stepped out. The father, never taking his eyes off the young woman, said quietly to his son, "Go get your mother."

Now that's a makeover. Put off. Put on. Take off the former way of life, and put on the life that God intends us to live. This lifelong commitment to growth doesn't just happen, however; it requires a certain kind of attitude.

The attitude of growth. So what is the attitudinal manner in which we should approach this makeover? How do we apply Paul's approach to discipline?

I am indebted to John Ortberg for a significant distinction that sheds much light on this. In his book *The Life You've Always Wanted,* Ortberg says that most of us have been *trying* to live the Christian life, instead of *training* to live the Christian life. There is an enormous difference between *trying* and *training.*[3]

What is the difference? A "trying" mentality is simply dabbling at something; you take a shot at it, but it's a short-term effort. You come at it from the mindset of, "Well, let's see what this is about," as if you are collecting experiences, but it is not pursued in depth. "Trying" is a life of flitting from one thing to another but landing nowhere.

There are many areas of life where a trying mentality simply will not cut it. No one would wake up on a Saturday morning, open the newspaper, notice that there is a marathon being held that day and then say, "Hey, I'm not doing anything today. I think I'll give it a try." It is obvious that months of careful, planned preparation are necessary to propel yourself across a twenty-six-mile course, regardless of the pace you set. You don't simply *try* to run a marathon, or play the piano, or become a doctor.

At some time in our life we have all had to face the fact that a training mentality is necessary to get us where we want to go; for most of us, for example, training has been required for our jobs or professions. The truth is that mastery of any skill requires dedicated hours of repetitious action.

This is the subject of Malcolm Gladwell's book *Outliers: The Story of Success.* He raises the issue of whether those who achieve significantly do it simply because they are more talented than others or because of other contributing factors. What he discovered is that talent is only one of the elements that leads to success. The formula is more like talent + preparation (perspiration) = achievement.

Gladwell focuses on what is called the ten-thousand-hour rule. Psychologists studied the students at Berlin's elite Academy of Music. They ended up dividing the students into three categories:

1. The stars: those with the potential to become concert violinists

2. The merely good

3. Those who would most likely end up teaching music in the public schools

What made the difference? It wasn't talent.

They simply asked all the students one question: Since you first picked up the violin, how many hours have you practiced? What they discovered was that the sheer number of hours of practice was what separated the students into these three categories. All the students started roughly at the age of five. By age twenty the future music teachers had practiced four thousand hours, the merely good had practiced eight thousand hours, but the ones who had the promise of being concert violinists had practiced ten thousand hours. They documented this ten-thousand-hour rule in a number of settings. Their conclusion: "It seems that it takes the brain that long to assimilate all that it needs to achieve true mastery."[4]

Pablo Casals, a world-renowned cellist in the early twentieth century, practiced five hours a day, even when he was recognized as the world's greatest at his instrument. I love the answer he gave when someone asked him why. He said, "I think I'm getting better."

If it takes this kind of effort to excel in the matters and skills of this world, how much more should we put into our training to fulfill the highest calling of becoming Christlike? Ortberg writes, "Spiritual transformation is not a matter of trying harder, but training wisely. . . . The need for preparation, or training, does not stop when it comes to learning the art of forgiveness, or joy, or courage. In other words, it applies to a healthy and vibrant spiritual life just as it does to physical and intellectual activity. Learning to think, feel, and act like Jesus is at least as demanding as learning to run a marathon or play the piano."[5]

The practice of growth. In introducing to us a rhythm of "put off, put on," Paul has already indicated the nature of this makeover. Look at the following words and phrases from Ephesians 4 and see if you can tell what they point to: "You must no longer *live* as the Gentiles do" (v. 17); "you, however, did not come to know Christ that *way*" (v. 20); "you were taught, with regard to your former *way of life*" (v. 22). What do the words *live, way, way of life* have in common? To what concept do they point? They state that the nature of life is about *habits*. To have a makeover is to change our habits of thinking, feeling and acting from a former way of life to our new identity in Christ. Interestingly enough, the word "habit" comes from the Latin *habitus,* which refers to the structure of the mind. It is like a piece of clothing that you put on—much the way those in religious orders wear *habits* as a sign that they are living a distinct way of life. Paul is essentially saying that Christian living is continuously making it our daily practice to put off the old habits and put on the new. This is our calling.

We are habitual creatures. We start by recognizing that we are creatures of habit. We have ways of thinking, feeling and acting that have become so second-nature to us that we don't even think about them. Habits are our unconscious practices.

I think back to the time when I first learned to drive a car. It was overwhelming. So many things to think about—put the key in the ignition, fasten the seat belt, move the seat into position, check the mirrors to see if they are the right angle, keep your eye on the speedometer, be aware of the traffic in front and back, and so on. I thought I'd never learn it all. I'm sure, if my father were alive today, he would remember quite well when I first sat behind the wheel of a car. He taught me to drive on a stick or manual shift. My father and I both prayed that, as we approached an intersection, the light would remain green. Mastering the standing start, especially on a hill, was more of an adventure than my father bargained for. Getting the right balance between releasing the clutch while giving it gas seemed almost impossible at the time; I don't know how many times I sent the car through the intersection heaving and lunging as if I were riding a bucking bronco. *Too many things to remember,* I thought. But countless hours later I can slip into a car in the black of midnight and find the slot for the ignition key while buckling my seat belt—all while carrying on a heated discussion about predestination.

So practically speaking, following Jesus is about training ourselves in the proper habits. We are full of God-displeasing habits of thinking, feeling and acting, which Paul calls our "former way of life" (Ephesians 4:22). We are to continuously put in place "the new self, created to be like God in true righteousness and holiness" (Ephesians 4:24).

Don't underestimate the grip of the old

habits. The reason we need a commitment to growth like that of an athlete is that changing habits is extremely hard. The habits that have become a part of us are integral to our automatic response system. Healthy or not, they have been absorbed into our bodies. When Paul tells the Ephesians, "No longer live as the Gentiles do," they could have replied, "But that's all we've ever known." The same is often true for us when our habits are confronted. We think, *This is the way we were raised.* And, in reality, all of us have been raised in families where the "you ares" have become "I ams": "You will never amount to anything." "You always do it wrong." "Why can't you be like your brother or sister?" These messages can become a part of us. In addition, we are immersed in a culture of images where the values of materialism (you are what you have) bombard us through TV, radio and film all the time. They shape our world and can become part of who we are as well.

Athletes of any stripe, even someone who's just a weekend golfer, know the difficulty of changing a bad habit. I can remember when I first heard the concept of "muscle memory"; it was a revelation to me. Athletes can practice bad habits. These bad habits then become part of our muscle memory; our muscles learn certain ways of doing things. When this happens, we might have to take some lessons and, as the pro observes our stroke, begin to teach our muscles a new motion. The new motion feels very awkward until we have done it over and over again, so that it becomes a part of our new structure.

This process of changing habits is something akin to gravitational pull. We have watched space shuttles launch into space, an occurrence that requires enormous thrust to break the gravitational pull of the earth's atmosphere. Most of the energy is spent in the first few minutes of lift-off, in the first few miles of travel. Similarly, breaking a habit takes a tremendous amount of effort. The power of the old habit wants to pull us back toward earth.

Why are habits so difficult to break? It is because they have sunk their roots deep into our lives in ways we do not even see. Have you ever tried to remove a tree stump? When spring comes you might say to yourself one Saturday afternoon, "I have a few minutes. I think I'll get that ugly stump out of the backyard." Three hours later you have dug a five-foot trench uncovering a network of roots that extends far deeper than you imagined. This is why the *trying* approach to the Christian life will leave you only frustrated. You have to be in it for the long haul if you want to become a true apprentice of Jesus.

Practice the principle of replacement. By laying out the framework of "putting off, putting on," Paul is giving us a very practical principle: the principle of replacement. We can't simply stop a bad habit; we have to put a new habit in its place. Why, for instance, do so many diets fail? Because we simply try to eat less, and the hunger pangs scream with a vengeance. In any area where we want to change—whether watching less TV, being less critical or sarcastic, or staying off those Internet sites that are not pleasing to God—unless we put something that is pleasing to God in place of the old habit, the old habit will actually come back with greater force, as in a story Jesus told about a man who had a demon cast from him. The demon went searching for a space to occupy. When it noticed that the man had not filled his life with a new center, it came back with seven other demons, and the man was worse off than before (see Luke 11:24-26).

To reinforce this principle of replacement, Paul gives five illustrations in Ephesians 4:25-32.

Clearly it is not sufficient to simply identify the thoughts, feelings or behaviors that need to be changed; they must be replaced with the biblical alternative.

How do we get in touch with the habits that need to be changed? It goes back to the spiritual practices or disciplines that I called "listening posts" in chapter three. We learn to listen to what God is saying and be attuned to our own lives through the Holy Spirit's work as we practice at least these four movements:

- Listening post 1: Place your life up next to the truth of Scripture.

- Listening post 2: Develop the discipline of solitude and silence in order to listen deeply.

- Listening post 3: Intertwine your life with trusted Christian friends who will help you live in truth.

- Listening post 4: Take faith risks by putting yourself in uncomfortable places.

The listening posts are simply illustrations of what we have come to call *spiritual disciplines*. Spiritual disciplines are the practices that we engage in to place ourselves in the presence of God in order to allow him to work on us. They are not—and I stress *not*—simply *willpower*. Any direct effort to change something by our willpower will only strengthen the very thing we are trying to change. Rather, spiritual disciplines are what we do to open ourselves to God and to his transforming work in us.

In his classic work *Celebration of Discipline,* Richard Foster describes the role of spiritual disciplines this way:

God has given us the Disciplines of the spiritual life as a means of receiving grace. The Disciplines allow us to place ourselves before God so that He can transform us. . . . By themselves the Spiritual Disciplines can

Table 1.

Verse	Put off	Put on
v. 25	falsehood	speaking truthfully
vv. 26-27	sinning in your anger	addressing issues quickly
v. 28	stealing	being useful with your hands
v. 29	unwholesome talk	building others up according to their needs
vv. 31-32	bitterness, rage, etc.	kindness, compassion and forgiveness

do nothing; they can only get us to the place where something can be done. They are God's means of grace. . . . God has ordained the Disciplines of the spiritual life as the means by which we are placed where He can bless us.[6]

For example, I show up daily to be in solitude and silence before God with my Bible, journal and pen in hand in order to sit quietly in conversation and dialogue with God over his Word. This discipline simply puts me where God can have his way with me. I also practice the rhythm of the prayer of examen so that God can show me what I need to see from yesterday's events, conversations and happenings; this discipline helps me learn to be aware of his presence in the moment. In addition, I regularly spend time serving locally in my community and internationally through missions trips to get out of my comfort zone and remind myself that this life is not about me but about God's heart for all peoples in all places. As Ortberg says, "Following Jesus simply means learning from him to arrange my life around activities that enable me to live in the fruit of the Spirit. . . . Spiritual disciplines are to life what practice is to a game."[7]

Here is how C. S. Lewis imagines what God intends to do when he invades our life. Consider yourself a living house, he says. God comes in to rebuild it. At first, he is doing the little stuff: unstopping the drains, fixing the leaks in the roof. These jobs have needed to be done, so you aren't surprised. But then God starts knocking the house about in a way that hurts. You wonder, What is God up to? The answer is that he is building a far different house out of you than the one you thought. He is throwing up a new wing here, an extra floor there, running up towers and making courtyards. You thought you were going to be a little decent cottage. He is building a palace. He intends to come and live in it himself.[8]

Loving God with all of our strength requires a training mentality, but it truly is far more challenging than running a marathon or mastering a musical instrument. We are to constantly be in the process of becoming reflectors of Christ's life in us, allowing him to shine through us.

---

[1]Dallas Willard, *The Great Omission: Reclaiming Jesus' Essential Teachings on Discipleship* (San Francisco: HarperSanFrancisco, 2006), p. 80.

[2]John Stott, *Basic Christianity* (Downers Grove, Ill.: InterVarsity Press, 2006), p. 159.

[3]John Ortberg, *The Life You've Always Wanted* (Grand Rapids: Zondervan, 1997), p. 47.

[4]Malcolm Gladwell, *Outliers: The Story of Success* (New York: Little, Brown, 2008), p. 35.

[5]Ortberg, *The Life You've Always Wanted*, p. 48

[6]Richard Foster, *Celebration of Discipline: The Path to Spiritual Growth* (San Francisco: Harper & Row, 1978), p. 13.

[7]Ortberg, *The Life You've Always Wanted*, p. 49.

[8]C. S. Lewis, *Mere Christianity* (New York: Macmillan, 1943), p. 174.

Reading Study Guide

1. Loving God with all of our strength is essentially the attitude Paul has in approaching the Christian life. How would you summarize this Pauline approach to living out our love for God?

2. Paul uses a "makeover" metaphor to describe the process of Christian growth. What do you understand Paul's "put off, put on" exhortation to mean?

3. What distinction does the reading make between *trying* and *training* in the Christian life?

4. Honestly, how would you characterize your attitude or approach to growing into Christ-likeness? On a scale of one to ten (with *trying* being one and *training* being ten), what number would you give yourself and why?

5. What is one habit of yours that you think the Lord is calling you to change in order to align yourself with God's character? It could be a habit of thinking, feeling or acting.

   How hard do you think it would be to change? Assess the difficulty.

6. What is the biblical alternative that you could put in place of that habit? Articulate as best as you can what your plan for change will be.

7. Go back to the list of listening posts. Is there one or more of these disciplines that you should adopt as a part of your regular rhythm of life?

8. What is a spiritual discipline?

What is it supposed to accomplish?

How do we keep it from becoming a law so that it remains a means of grace?

Going Deeper

Ortberg, John. *The Life You've Always Wanted.* Grand Rapids: Zondervan, 1997. Ortberg describes this book as "Dallas Willard lite." Essentially it's an introduction to the spiritual disciplines. His chapter on trying versus training is worth the price of the book, as he lays out the approach we must take if we're to bring ourselves into the attitude necessary for Christlike transformation.

9 / Growing Healthy Bodies

LOOKING AHEAD

MEMORY VERSES: 1 Corinthians 6:19-20
BIBLE STUDY: Selected Scriptures on the theme of "God's Dwelling Place"
READING: Our Bodies as God's Temple

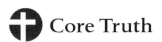 **Core Truth**

What role does the body have in our loving God?

There are two opposite errors we tend to make regarding the body. On the one hand, at times in Christian history we have adopted a wrongheaded asceticism that assumes the body is inherently evil and therefore is to be punished through rigid self-denial. On the other hand, the current error is to worship the body as an end in itself which leads to a life of sensuality and self-gratification. Biblically the body is the dwelling place of the Holy Spirit. The body is to be released to the Spirit's control and discipline so that our natural inclinations are brought in line with God's impulses.

1. Identify key words or phrases in the question and answer above, and state their meaning in your own words.

2. Restate the core truth in your own words.

3. What questions or issues does the core truth raise for you?

Memory Verse Study Guide

Our Scripture memory verses take us to Paul's classic statement of the place of the body in our spiritual life. In the midst of addressing the mores of sexual immorality that dominated pagan Greek culture and worship, Paul teaches us about the Lord's relationship to our bodies as well as what it means to view our bodies as instruments of righteousness.

1. *Putting it in context:* Read 1 Corinthians 6:12-18. Restate in your own words the argument that Paul makes against the sexual immorality of uniting our bodies with a prostitute.

2. The memory verses are *1 Corinthians 6:19-20*. Copy the verses verbatim.

3. Take some time to meditate on Paul's statement, "Your body is a temple of the Holy Spirit." What feelings does this evoke in you?

   What are some of the implications of this statement for the way we are to live our lives?

4. Paul writes, "You are not your own; you were bought at a price." How do we reconcile a statement like this with the fact that one of the fruits of the Spirit is self-control or self-mastery, as we learned in the last chapter? Can both be true? If so, in what way?

5. How do we "honor God with [our] body"?

   In a spirit of confession, think about how you might currently be dishonoring God with your body. What change might the Lord be asking you to make to bring your bodily response in line with your inner loyalty to God?

Inductive Bible Study Guide

In this study, we will depart from the usual examination of one passage of Scripture in order to trace the development of the theme of the "dwelling place of God among his people." As we trace this theme through the old and new covenant we will see the presence of God identified with the tabernacle and temple through the ark of the covenant; the imagery of God's presence ultimately expressed in the incarnation of Jesus Christ as the God-man; and then finally how the Spirit of Jesus (the Holy Spirit) continues to dwell on earth, resident in his people. This provides the basis needed for us to see the merger of God's Spirit with our bodies as the temple of God.

1. Under the old covenant, the tabernacle and temple are considered the visual place of God's residence on earth. God's presence is associated with the ark of the covenant in particular.

   a. *Read Exodus 25:1-22.* What does this passage on the construction of the tabernacle teach us about where God dwells and, in particular, the association of his presence with the ark of the covenant?

   b. *Read 1 Kings 8:1-13.* King Solomon, King David's son, was given the right to build a more permanent dwelling place for God—the temple—in contrast to the mobile tabernacle. How is the significance of this location stated at the temple's dedication?

2. Jesus Christ becomes the dwelling place of God on earth.

   a. *Read John 1:1, 14.* How does John's language here indicate that Jesus is the fulfillment of the Old Testament images related to the tabernacle and temple?

   b. *Read John 2:12-22.* Jesus had a particular passion for the temple as his Father's dwelling place. When he saw how it was being abused, holy rage was manifested. In verses 19-22, how does Jesus shift the temple image to himself?

What is the significance of this?

3. Finally, the people of God—the church—have become the new temple in whom God dwells. Jesus sends the Holy Spirit, his presence, to live in us.

a. *Read 1 Corinthians 3:10-17.* Paul completes the temple imagery. Where does God now dwell upon the earth?

What are the implications of this truth?

b. *Read Galatians 2:20.* How does Paul express the merging of divinity and humanity?

4. How does the study of this thematic development deepen your appreciation for the nature of our spiritual life and the place of the church in God's scheme?

⚭ Reading: Our Bodies as God's Temple

In chapter eight we said that loving God with all of our strength requires disciplining our spirit and body. We began to touch on the reality that our bodies are an integral part of the totality of what it means to be soulful persons. From the beginning when God first breathed his life (soul) into man whom he made from the dust of the earth, we see the total intermingling of body and soul (Genesis 2:7).

In this chapter, we want to succinctly answer two questions. First, what is the Christian or biblical view of the body? And second, how does the body become the outer expression of the inwardly changed life?

To answer these questions, we must first correct an error that has seeped into and become a part of our popular worldview regarding the body. We have inadvertently adopted a Greek dualist perspective that contradicts the biblical understanding of the body.

The Greeks considered the body a lower order of existence. The material world was of a lesser nature than the spiritual world. In other words, the soul and the body existed in totally separate realms with the soul elevated over the body. (See chapter five, page 79, to recall the Greek view of the body and the soul.)

I cannot say strongly enough that this is *not* the biblical teaching about the body and the soul. It's not found anywhere in the biblical worldview. Rather, it's been imported from this outside source. Yet it has been repeated so often that it has pervaded the Christian consciousness.

THE INSEPARABILITY OF BODY AND SOUL

When we look at the body and soul through the lens of Scripture, we see a far different picture.

It has been said that Christianity is the most *material* of all the religions. By using the term *material,* though, I don't mean materialism. Materialism is reducing the meaning of life to the acquisition of material possessions: you are what you have. Rather, to say that Christianity is material means that the body and its means of sustenance are vital and integral to personhood. As Lewis Smedes writes, "The body is the person turned outward."[1] In other words, the body matters—a lot. We can't imagine life without our bodies. And there is nothing about the body that is inherently evil or of a lesser order of existence. To be created in the image of God is to be created as bodily persons (Genesis 1:26-27).

Moreover, at the very heart of our faith is the belief that we have been visited by God in human form in the person of Jesus Christ—"God in a body," we might say. Jesus becoming human was not condescension to a lower order of existence. To become a bodily being was not to intrinsically take on a substandard existence or something that was by its very nature sinful. In fact, the Scripture says that Jesus was tempted in all ways like us but was without sin (Hebrews 4:15). Jesus was fully human, yet he lived a perfect life. So to be human does not mean to be corrupt.

In our inductive Bible study in this chapter, I asked you to trace the development of the idea of the dwelling place of God among humanity. I won't repeat that in detail here, but let me just give a brief summary. The apostle John's identification of Jesus as the Word made flesh who "tabernacled among us" is a direct allusion to the tabernacle and temple as the dwelling place of God under the Old Covenant. John assumes these images, affirming that Jesus is "Immanuel, God with us" (see Matthew 1:23). John goes on to further underscore this connection with the temple by stating that "we have seen [Jesus'] glory, the glory of the One and Only, who came from the Father, full of grace and truth" (John 1:14). Then Jesus himself makes the direct connection between himself and the temple when he zealously cleanses the physical temple of the money changers and then asserts that in three days he will raise up the temple, referring to his own body (John 2:12-22). Finally, we saw that this imagery is ultimately fulfilled when Jesus sends his replacement, the Holy Spirit, who dwells among his people, the new temple of God on earth (1 Corinthians 3:16-17; 6:19-20).

The implication of this last point is that the Holy Spirit has sanctified—made holy—we who are sinful people so that God's presence can occupy our very bodies. Admittedly, Paul is painting a corporate picture of the church as the dwelling place of God—but the church is, after all, made up of each of us as individuals, indwelt in our bodies by the Spirit.

THE FUTURE OF OUR BODIES

In a moment we will get back to the implications of our bodies being the dwelling place of God for holy living, but first let's consider the future of our bodily existence. Our understanding of what happens at death tends to look like the Greek view of the body. But what really occurs to these bodies when we die? Are they cast aside as a lower order of existence? Do we become purely ethereal soulish creatures with no physical substance?

To adopt a Pauline retort, "By no means!" As Smedes notes, "The body, for Paul, is not a piece of fleshly baggage that can be dropped to allow the soul to float aloft in freedom. A person is not a soul wrapped in a fleshly package."[2] In Paul's extended discussion of the importance of the resurrection in 1 Corinthians 15, he captures both the continuity and discontinuity of our physical existence in our resurrected state. He says on the one hand that we will indeed have a bodily existence eternally, what he calls a "spiritual body." In other words, our bodies will continue to exist in some fashion.

What will not continue, however, is the limitations of our bodies in their current form. These limitations exist only because our rebellious state has affected our bodies. So, we get tired, hungry and thirsty. We need to be continuously replenished.

We are subject to the temptations of the body, pandering to desires that sometimes seem to have a separate life of their own. Our bodies cannot sustain the glory of God after moments of a spiritual high or in-depth communion. We want to mingle, as C. S. Lewis says, with the glories we see, but we cannot. Even moments of human pleasure, like a delicious meal, a great movie or deep human conversation, cannot be held on to because we are trapped in time. In our sinful and fallen state, the original intent for our bodies has been impacted. However, in our resurrected bodies, these limitations will be discontinued. As we enter a new order of reality, our mortal, limited bodies will take on immorality and will have a new substance that can hold the glory of God and remain forever. The body will be restored to be all God originally intended it to be.

Paul deploys analogous language in an attempt to describe the new order of glory that will be ours: "So will it be with the resurrection of the dead. The body that is sown is perishable, it is raised imperishable; it is sown in dishonor, it is raised in glory; it is sown in weakness, it is raised in power; it is sown a natural body, it is raised a spiritual body" (1 Corinthians 15:42-44). His description makes it clear that our bodies themselves are not inherently evil or a lesser order of life from the beginning. Rather, so integral is this bodily existence to our nature that we will be redeemed eternally in some imperishable, glorious bodily form hinted at by Paul.

The resurrection of Jesus gives a little window into the powers that our bodies will have when we enter this new realm of redemption and illustrates for us both the continuity and discontinuity that Paul articulates in his teaching in 1 Corinthians 15. Paul calls Jesus "the firstfruits of those who have fallen asleep [died]" (1 Corinthians 15:20). In other words, Jesus is the "firstfruits" of the "harvest" of the resurrection to come, of which we'll also be a part. What can we learn about our resurrection from Jesus' resurrection?

Scripture makes it clear, first off, that Jesus emerged from the tomb and walked this earth for some forty days in a real, physical body. But his body was different; he took on new powers that he either chose not to display or did not have prior to his resurrection. For example, when Jesus entered the locked upper room where his fearful disciples were staying, he didn't walk through an open door; he just appeared (John 20:19). On another occasion, two of his followers whom he met and walked with on the road to Emmaus didn't recognize him until he broke bread with them. Jesus' physical appearance in his resurrected state had apparently been altered sufficiently that he did not seem like the same person they had known prior to his resurrection. Then, just as suddenly as "their eyes were opened," Jesus vanished—and appeared among the other disciples just as these same two were explaining what had just taken place (Luke 24:28-39). At first his disciples thought that they must be seeing a ghost. But Jesus went to great pains to assure them that, in his resurrected state, he was still quite substantive: "He said to them, 'Why are you troubled, and why do doubts rise in your minds? Look at my hands and my feet. It is I myself! Touch me and see; a ghost does not have flesh and bones, as you see I have." Then to further convince them that they did not have "lying eyes," Jesus asked for something to eat. Luke records that "they gave him a piece of broiled fish, and he took it and ate it in their presence" (Luke 24:42-43).

If Jesus is our model of what the resurrected state might look like, we can have faith that we too will have a bodily existence complete with new powers in our resurrection.

Our Bodies as God's Temple

Let's consider now two major discipleship implications for us as bodily beings. First, we need to treat our physical bodies with reverence. Second, we are exhorted to present our bodies as instruments of righteousness.

Physical health. One of the ways the Greek dualistic "body versus spirit" manifests itself today is in our disassociation of the spiritual life from the way we treat our bodies. Author and spiritual director Ruth Haley Barton describes struggles she's faced with this trap: "Intent on trying to be 'spiritual,' for years I thought my body warranted little attention. As long as warning lights weren't flashing, I could ignore it in favor of more spiritual endeavors— silence and solitude, Scripture and prayer, service and self-denial."[3] She came to dis-

cover that the physical and the spiritual were "inescapably intertwined." Dorothy Bass concurs, writing, "As the place where the divine presence dwells, our bodies are worthy of care and blessing and ought never to be degraded or exploited. It is through our bodies that we participate in God's activity in the world."[4]

If we are to love God with all of our strength and see our bodies as the temple of the Holy Spirit, wouldn't this include treating our bodies with the utmost care? Shouldn't we be maximizing our physical health in order to focus the entirety of our energy toward service to the God we say we love? Can we love God and mistreat our bodies? Shouldn't believers be the healthiest of all people, because of having reverence for our bodies? Let's takes some time to reconsider the common elements that must be addressed to maximize our bodily health: diet, exercise and rest.

Diet. It matters what we put into our bodies. As a cancer survivor I have become even more aware of how our diet (eating regimen) impacts our immune system, which is what gives our bodies the ability to fight off disease. To the extent that we eat an unhealthy diet, we compromise our body's ability to do what it is designed to do. It has been generally shown that a diet high in colorful fruits and vegetables and appropriate grains provides the necessary ingredients for maximizing the body's health.[5] But the issue for most of us is not that we need more information about healthy eating habits; it is the will and conviction to do what is right.

As I have become more health conscious over the last thirty years, I have gone through a major transformation as to what goes into my body. As a twenty- and thirtysomething my palate thrived on the usual American meat and potatoes diet, supplemented by fast-food offerings of burgers and fries. Ordering fish at a restaurant? Why would I waste my money on that! Over the years, though, the very foods I would have gagged on in the past have become the things I am drawn to and enjoy. Now when I think of putting French fries—or a burger that contains a whole day's worth of calories—into my body, I say to myself, *Why would I want to put poison into my system?* Eating, I've come to learn, is like any habit. We can be trained to like new foods that allow the body to release its own inherent power the way that God has designed it.

Exercise. The body is made up of a number of systems (skeletal, digestive, circulatory, nervous) that can all be improved in their functioning by keeping our cardiovascular system healthy. Keeping our heart healthy and our metabolism as high as possible feeds the strength of the rest of the body's systems.

It took me some time to find a fitness program that was right for me. Since I view exercise as an opportunity for renewal that has as much benefit emotionally and spiritually as it does physically, I pursue it largely as a solitary experience. Others I know see exercise as a social outlet. Having partners with whom to share the experience can enhance the discipline and provide a shared bond.

I am also aware—from firsthand experience—that some of us (like myself) love the perspiration that comes with a good workout, while others (like my wife) just are not naturally drawn to strenuous physical engagement. My wife says, "I do it because I know it's good for me, but don't ask me to like it." She's glad when her morning strength-training class is finished so that it can be checked off the day's to-do list and is not "hanging over her head" the rest of the day. I, on the other hand, anticipate and look forward to my late afternoon opportunity for solitude and a strenuous workout. After thirty-three years of regular physical exercise, it is built into my lifestyle, and it allows me to be renewed at the end of the day and release any accumulated frustrations. Even when I come home dragging a bit after work and say to myself, "I don't feel like working out today," more often than not, I usually do, because the momentum of the discipline carries me. Good habits, just like bad habits, have their own impetus.

Rest. God has built into the rhythm of life rest from our toil. It's called Sabbath. The Designer created the body with a need for regular renewal—and he himself serves as the model for this pattern: "By the seventh day God had finished the work he had been doing; so on the seventh day he rested from all his work. And God blessed the seventh day and made it holy, because on it he rested from all the work of creating that he had done" (Genesis 2:2-3). So humans are designed to set aside a weekly Sabbath to disconnect from our labor and be refreshed in the Lord. In this sense, the Sabbath is not only about rest but also about perspective, helping us separate our identity from our work. We are the Lord's; our work is simply one expression of who we are. As Jesus reminded his antagonists who wanted to turn the Sabbath into a stultifying, legalistic observance, God gave the Sabbath as a gift, not a straitjacket: "The Sabbath was made for man, not man for the Sabbath" (Mark 2:27). Don't deny yourself this gift of rest that renews and reminds you whose you are.

Whether it's daily rest, or the weekly rhythm of the Sabbath, or refreshing quarterly days of solitude and silence, or an annual retreat, our bodies and spirits need the renewal that comes with rest. And, even more broadly, the combination of diet, exercise and rest provides our bodies with the possibility of being at the optimum availability for loving God with all of our strength.

Our bodies as instruments of righteousness. In 1 Corinthians 6:12-20, Paul spells out further implications of our bodies being the temple of the Holy Spirit, particularly in the area of sexual immorality. In the Corinthian culture, attaching your body to a prostitute was part of the religious activity in the pagan temples. Paul shows that this is an act of sin against your own body and against the Lord who occupies the body. The sexual act, as Paul makes clear in chapter 7 when he writes on marriage, is a gift of God to be expressed in the context of the one-flesh union of a man and a woman. To attach one's body to a prostitute as an act of worship is to take what God has intended for deep communion between a husband and wife, denigrate it through a casual union and then try to justify it as a religious activity.

When we become believers, our bodies become united with Christ himself. Everything we do with our bodies must therefore be seen in light of the fact that we are members of him. We must treat our bodies as temples in which he dwells. Here is how Paul puts it in Romans 6:12-14:

> Therefore do not let sin reign in your mortal body so that you obey its evil desires. Do not offer the parts of your body to sin, as instruments of wickedness, but rather offer yourselves to God, as those who have been brought from death to life; and offer the parts of your body to him as instruments of righteousness. For sin shall not be your master, because you are not under law, but under grace.

In other words, flowing through our bodies are two life forces that are in conflict. Prior to Christ, our desire was to use our bodies for that which did not please God. The momentum was all in the direction of self-consumption. Then, in Christ, the life force of grace invaded our bodies and intends to take over the deep impulses of our life. In a very practical way, our bodies indicate to us what areas need further relinquishment. The apostle James, for example, speaks of the tongue as an unruly member

(James 3:1-12); our speech can be a direct indicator of what needs to be changed in us. At times our bodies may be dominated by feelings of rage, anger or resentment—feelings that are related to emotional memories lodged in our bodies. I personally have had a lifelong battle with fear, which I experience as a clutch in the stomach. When we pay attention to the messages from our bodies, the Lord speaks to us about what needs to be changed. The inner life is manifested outwardly in our bodies.

In the introduction I referenced Dallas Willard and his suggestion that the goal of our loving God is to have our beings so responsive to the impulses of God's heart that we have an *embedded* will; in other words, we become so attuned with the heart of God that we move beyond sheer retrospective reflection on how the Lord would have had us respond and are instead under the control of God's impulses in the moment. This cannot be done without the full engagement of our bodies in the process. We pray, for instance, with varied postures—on our knees, face down to the floor, hands held high—all to express in our bodies the attitude of our spirit. The spiritual disciplines referenced in our last chapter are all disciplines of the body as well. As Paul says, "The body is . . . meant . . . for the Lord, and the Lord for the body. . . . Therefore honor God with your body" (1 Corinthians 6:13, 20). Spirituality is lived out in our bodies.

Here (in summary fashion) are four practical steps Willard suggests we can take regarding our bodies:[6]

1. *Release your body to God.* Visualize offering each part of your body and its purposes to God as a vehicle through which he can work.

2. *No longer idolize the body.* Do not treat it as an object of "ultimate concern" as most of us tend to do in our current culture.

3. *Do not misuse the body.* Don't abuse the body through poor diet or addictive practices, or use it to control others through sexual manipulation or domineering actions.

4. *Properly honor and care for the body.* In other words, follow a proper diet, exercise and engage in restful practices to optimize the body's capacity.

CONCLUSION

To live out our love for God with all of our strength, we must embrace our bodies as a significant element of our identity. Toward this aim, Willard recounts for us a story: "A priest once said to Meister Eckhardt: 'I wish that your soul were in my body.' To which he replied, 'You would really be foolish. That would get you nowhere—it would accomplish little for your soul to be in my body. No soul can really do anything except through the body to which it is attached.'"[7]

The body in Christian teaching, then, is not something that is inherently of a lower order of existence or by its nature sinful. We do not make a distinction between body and soul as if each can be kept in its own airtight compartment. They are commingled: to be soulful is to be bodily. Moreover, we are to embrace our bodies as the habitation of God. The Holy Spirit has honored us by taking up residence in us, having declared us righteous through the work of Christ. Now God seeks to glorify himself in our bodies as we offer them to him, presenting them as "living sacrifices" (see Romans 12:1) for his good work.

---

[1]Lewis B. Smedes, *Union with Christ* (Grand Rapids: Eerdmans, 1970), p. 162.

[2]Ibid., p. 161.

[3]Ruth Haley Barton, "Flesh-and-Blood Spirituality," *Re:generation Quarterly,* April 1, 1999, p. 13.

[4]Dorothy C. Bass, quoted in ibid.

[5]The USDA (United States Department of Agriculture) has created a food pyramid that highlights the appropriate priorities for our proper nutrition. See <www.usda.gov> for more information.

[6]Dallas Willard, *Renovation of the Heart* (Colorado Springs: NavPress, 2002), pp. 172-74.

[7]Dallas Willard, *The Spirit of the Disciplines* (San Francisco: Harper & Row, 1988), p. 82.

Reading Study Guide

1. What is the false understanding of the nature of the body that has infiltrated Christian teaching?

2. How would you summarize Christian teaching about the nature of the body?

3. How do the incarnation of Jesus—where he fully became a man—and his subsequent bodily resurrection affirm the importance of the body?

4. Based on Jesus' resurrection, what do you think our resurrection bodies will be like?

5. Do you agree or disagree with the idea that our Christian practice has tended to separate our understanding of the spiritual life from the care and importance of our body? Explain your answer.

6. Up to this point in your life, what has been your understanding of the connection between Christian discipleship and personal physical health?

7. What steps are you convicted to take to enhance the connection between your discipleship and personal health?

8. In 1 Corinthians 6:12-20, Paul says that our bodies are members of Christ. What implications does he draw in this passage for the way we use our bodies?

9. Where is your body sending you a message that indicates you need further relinquishment in order to offer that part to God as an "instrument of righteousness"?

10. What have you learned in the last two chapters about how the body is to be brought in line with our love for God?

Going Deeper

Barton, Ruth Haley. *Sacred Rhythms.* Downers Grove, Ill.: IVP Books, 2006. As an excellent supplement to this chapter, read chapter five, "Honoring the Body: Flesh-and-Blood Spirituality."

Part Five

LOVE YOUR NEIGHBOR AS YOURSELF

In answer to the question posed to Jesus, "Of all the commandments, which is the most important?" he, in fact, offers two commandments: "Love the Lord your God" and "Love your neighbor as yourself." Essentially, Jesus is saying that these two commandments are inseparable and therefore must be treated as one. He could not imagine loving God without loving your neighbor; the natural outflow of our love for God will be our growing capacity to love our neighbor.

At the outset, we must address a common misinterpretation of what it means to "love your neighbor as yourself." In our age, when we think low self-esteem is the root of all of humankind's problems, we have stressed loving ourselves as the means to loving our neighbor. Common therapeutic wisdom backs us up here, telling us that we can't love others if we do not love ourselves. I suppose there is some truth to that, but this can and often does lead us to emphasize the "as yourself" part more than love for our neighbor. When we do this, we actually turn Jesus' response into three commands, not two, and twist his words around to mean, "Love yourself as the way to grow in love for neighbor." This is not what Jesus is saying.

Jesus' words here about "loving ourselves" are not a command. Rather, he is stating a reality. No one has to tell us to look out for ourselves. What he's calling us to do is to *love our neighbor in the same way* that we already love ourselves. Paul states this in a different way when he addresses the husband-wife relationship, but he makes exactly the same point as Jesus: taking into account our own self-interest is second nature to every human being. "In this same way, husbands ought to love their wives as their own bodies," Paul writes. "He who loves his wife loves himself. After all, no one ever hated his own body, but he feeds and cares for it" (Ephesians 5:28-29). A preacher I recently heard put it well: "I don't have to wake up every morning and exhort myself, 'Take care of me.' This is our bent; the way it is." Jesus is simply saying, "Put in as much energy into loving your neighbor as you do in taking care of yourself."

In this final section, we will explore three dimensions of what it means to "love your neighbor." Chapter ten explores the obvious question at hand, "Who is my neighbor?" This is the question posed by the teacher of the law in an attempt to limit his obligation, and it prompted one of the most well-known parables of Jesus, that of the good Samaritan. In the parable Jesus defines *neighbor* as anyone in proximity with a need that we could help, so the key word for this chapter is *mercy*.

Then in chapter eleven we raise the bar even higher, because Jesus expands on the definition of *neighbor* by calling us to also *love our enemies* and do good to those who persecute us. This chapter takes us into one of the most difficult interplays that followers of Jesus must deal with: love versus justice. Jesus is saying that love supersedes justice. When we are wronged, everything in our being wants to redress the wrong; we must have justice! Yet Jesus tells us that there is a higher law, the law of love. In this chapter we will deal with both how we handle personal grievances and how Jesus' teaching on nonviolent, loving resistance has been applied to societal injustice.

Finally, we conclude in chapter twelve with a look at the biblical emphasis on demonstrating our love for God by our love for our neighbor. The Scripture raises the question, Can you possibly love God and not demonstrate it through a life of compassionate service to those around you? We will explore the biblical incongruity of saying that we love God while not loving our neighbor, as well as the powerful force of *compassion* on a personal and social level as evidenced in the life of Jesus.

10 / Have Mercy for Those in Need

LOOKING AHEAD

MEMORY VERSES: Matthew 9:12-13
BIBLE STUDY: Mark 10:46-52
READING: Scandalous Love

 Core Truth

Who is my neighbor?

Jesus throws open the door as wide as possible when it comes to the identity of our neighbor. He explodes the barriers of race, economic condition, ethnic origin, ideological persuasion, legal status and so on to include any who are in need that we might have the resources and wherewithal to do anything about. Mercy is the critical link between our hearts and those who are in need.

1. Identify key words or phrases in the question and answer above, and state their meaning in your own words.

2. Restate the core truth in your own words.

3. What questions or issues does the core truth raise for you?

Memory Verse Study Guide

The people Jesus hung out with were a constant embarrassment to the powerful who thought they defined the standards of righteousness. The keepers of the morals of society saw the people Jesus associated with as those who watered down the moral "gene pool." In our memory verses, Jesus turns righteousness on its head and equates it not with upstanding behavior but with mercy.

1. *Putting it in context:* Read Matthew 9:9-11. Try to look at those who gathered at Matthew's home through the eyes of the Pharisees. How would you describe what they observed?

2. The memory verses are *Matthew 9:12-13*. Copy the verses verbatim.

3. How do you think Jesus is using the words *healthy* and *righteous* in this setting?

   Are there any who could be considered "healthy" and "righteous"? Explain.

4. What is Jesus' critique of the Pharisees in this setting?

5. What does Jesus mean when he says, "I desire mercy, not sacrifice"?

6. What are the implications here for us if we are to follow Jesus' heart and model?

✎ Inductive Bible Study Guide

Jesus embodied and enacted the mercy that he told the Pharisees to adopt. Our Bible study passage is one specific example of a common interaction that Jesus had with those in need. He was continuously allowing his travels to be "interrupted" by the needs of those who sought his help. In this passage we meet a blind beggar by the name of Bartimaeus who would not be denied help when Jesus passed by. In Jesus he saw his one opportunity to have what he thought was never possible—his sight.

1. *Read Mark 10:46-52.* Blind Bartimaeus is sitting in his usual location as a beggar. When he hears that Jesus is passing by, he calls out to him. What had Bartimaeus concluded was true about this man whose help he was seeking?

2. Many in the crowd try to silence Bartimaeus when he cries out, "Jesus, Son of David, have mercy on me!" What does his persistence tell us about his state of mind?

3. When Bartimaeus is brought to Jesus at his request, Jesus asks him a question that seems to have an obvious answer: "What do you want me to do for you?" Why would it be important for Jesus to ask this question?

4. How would you answer that question for yourself right now? What do you want Jesus to do for you?

5. Jesus did for Bartimaeus what was in his power to do for him. He gave him his sight in response to his faith. Is there a need in your immediate network of relationships that

you have the power to do something about, but have not followed through on—maybe a Bartimaeus whose voice continues to haunt you? Name at least one need or person who comes to mind.

What might be keeping you from addressing that need?

👓 Reading: Scandalous Love

Any discussion of what it means to "love your neighbor as yourself" must begin with what we have come to call "The Parable of the Good Samaritan," which is Jesus' response to the self-justifying question of the expert in the law, "Who is my neighbor?"

The parable has generally been turned into a story that has a nice moralistic message, with the thrust usually being an ethical exhortation to "do good to those in need." This makes the parable fodder for those who like to reduce Christianity to a set of norms, divorced from the person of Christ. "It's the teaching of Jesus that's important, not his person," we hear people say. Or, "It's what he stood for that's his legacy; worshiping the man is not what he intended." People separate the person of Christ from what he taught and equate Christianity with the ethical norm found in many religions: "Do unto others as you would have others do unto you."

But when we see this story in its context, in the drama of the theological dialogue that transpires between the lawyer and Jesus, the parable takes on new light. It cannot be separated from the person of Jesus, nor is there any Christianity without the ongoing worship and following of the crucified and resurrected Savior.

The story, recorded in Luke 10, is told as a response to a debate that has two rounds.[1] Within each round there are two questions asked and two answers given.

Each round concludes with Jesus giving a similar exhortation to the lawyer to do what he says he believes: "Do this and you will live" (v. 28) and "Go and do likewise" (v. 37). I want you to see the symmetry of a very intentional structure.

ROUND ONE

"On one occasion an expert in the law stood up to test Jesus. 'Teacher,' he asked, 'what must I do to inherit eternal life?'" (v. 25). Notice, first, the mindset or motivation behind the lawyer's question. His standing to ask a question is an act of respect, but it masks an inner deception. He is not an innocent, sincere questioner seeking an answer that has long eluded him. As a lawyer or scribe, his whole professional life would have been devoted to applying the law to all facets of life. And the scribes, as we noted in chapter one, had identified 613 laws to which they had overtly committed themselves as a sign of their faithfulness to God.

Lawyers were into words, thriving on theological fencing matches and the repartee that came with intellectual debate about the fine points of applying the law to the miniscule details of life. They loved nothing better than holding a high-level conference of rabbis to debate whether the garden vegetables of mint, dill and cummin should be included in their tithe. Talking something to death was a way of life. So this certainly is the lawyer's intent when he stands to ask Jesus, "Teacher, what shall I do to inherit eternal life?"

He also already has the right answer in mind. Jesus had a reputation for playing footloose with the law. His practice of healing and allowing his disciples to pick grain on the Sabbath, for example, was a disturbing trend—particularly for those like the lawyer who believed keeping the law was the way to inherit eternal life. Rabbi Hillel, for example, a well-known teacher of the law who preceded Jesus by a generation, taught that he "who has gained the words of the Torah has gained for himself eternal life." Note even the internal contradiction in the question "What must I do to inherit eternal life?" An inheritance is a gift; there is nothing you can do to attain it. But the position of the lawyer was that rule keeping—following the law— was the prerequisite for life forever. He is trying to trap Jesus in the act of undermining the law.

In addition to already having the correct answer in mind, the lawyer had probably anticipated the kind of response Jesus might give and therefore had his retort in mind too. Then the fencing match would begin. What he hadn't counted on is Jesus' refusal to play the game. Jesus almost insultingly turns the question back on the lawyer: "'What is written in the Law?' he replied. 'How do you read it?'" (v. 26). Jesus is essentially saying, "This is your profession. It's part of your everyday thinking to put your mind to eternal things. What does your study tell you?" He responds with a question to a question. (This same

pattern is repeated in the second round.)

The lawyer's answer goes to the heart of the law. He combines references to Deuteronomy 6:5 and Leviticus 19:18: "'Love the Lord your God with all your heart and with all your soul and with all your strength and with all your mind'; and, 'Love your neighbor as yourself'" (v. 27). Jesus, as we know from the Gospels of Matthew and Mark, had cited this same combination of verses as a summary of the whole law in response to the religious legalist's challenge to him. Perhaps this lawyer had heard Jesus' insightful summary and is now trying to flatter Jesus by feeding it back to him.

Jesus then answers the lawyer's first question about eternal life: "You have answered correctly. . . . Do this, and you will live" (v. 28). End of discussion. No debate. Jesus, knowing how the lawyers tended to operate (as the saying goes, "When all is said and done, there is a lot more said than done"), is basically saying to them, "We are not going to talk this to death as if talking about it means you have done something. Cut the talk, and just do it."

On the surface, "Do this, and you will live" is a disturbing response by Jesus. It appears that Jesus is buying into the legalist's framework, where eternal life is the byproduct of leading a loving, ethical life. Is Jesus affirming that life forever is based on a person's ability to fully love God and our neighbor?

For the time being I believe Jesus is saying, "OK, let's take your position and see where it leads. You want to do something to inherit eternal life? Very well. Just continuously love God and your neighbor with the totality of who you are." In this sense, Jesus and the apostle Paul agreed with their contemporaries: complete obedience to the law of God is the way to be made right with God.

The problem is that, in experience, no human being can achieve complete obedience to the law. This is because the purpose of the law is not to save but to show us our need for a savior; it's not to cause us to redouble our efforts to somehow reach for the stars but to drive us to our knees in despair. The law is an expression of the holiness of God, which automatically shows us how far short we fall, and it contains no power to help us become holier. Therefore, the law only makes us more miserable—which is what it is intended to do.

Jesus is therefore placing a limitless demand on the lawyer, drawing no lines to tell him when he has done this fully. He lets the impossible standards of the law suspend in midair without qualification, waiting for the lawyer to see the sheer impossibility of keeping the entire law.

ROUND TWO

But the lawyer is not giving up yet. Instead of casting himself on God's mercy, he wants to limit the law and define what's attainable. He can't live with this open-ended, all-encompassing standard of holiness. Rather, he wants a definable list to accomplish so that he can declare himself righteous. From this heart-stance the lawyer poses the first question of the second round in his attempted theological fencing match: "But he wanted to justify himself, so he asked Jesus, 'And who is my neighbor?'" (v. 29). The lawyer is essentially saying, "I don't want to rush into anything. What if I went out and loved someone who turned out not to be my neighbor? I think we need to study this, and have a conference on it."

In Jesus' day there was, in fact, much lively debate within the scribal community on this very subject. You could easily imagine the Greater Jerusalem Scribal University publishing a festschrift to the late Rabbi Hillel on the subject, "who is my neighbor?" The conclusion they had come to was that "neighbors" were fellow Jews and maybe proselytes—God-fearing Gentiles who had converted to Judaism—but not Gentiles in general. The rabbis taught, for example, that it was wrong to contrive the death of a Gentile, but if a Gentile was in danger of dying because of some accident, you need not help the person, because "such a one is not thy neighbor."

Again, the lawyer is looking for a clear definition of who his neighbor is so that he can say, "I have loved fully; I have met my obligation." As Luke implies in verse 29, he is a prime example of self-justification: having a clearly defined standard that, once reached, allows a person to say to themselves, "Approved."

So when the lawyer asks, "Who is my neighbor?" he wants to start another round of theological debate that will clearly define who can be on his list.

As in round one, Jesus responds with a question, but this one comes at the end of his parable about the good Samaritan. Note how, in his story, Jesus turns the question around, asking, "Which of these three do you think was a neighbor to the man who fell into the hands of robbers?" (v. 36). He's not answering, "Who is my neighbor?" but "To whom am I willing to be a neighbor?" Thomas Walter Manson's observation is apropos: "The lawyer's question is unanswerable and ought not to be asked. For love does not begin by defining its objects, it discovers them."[2]

THE PARABLE OF THE GOOD SAMARITAN

To set up his new question, Jesus tells us a story with a number of scenes.

Scene one: The victim. We are first introduced to a victim: "A man was going down from Jerusalem to Jericho, when he fell into the hands of robbers. They stripped him of his clothes, beat him and went away, leaving him half dead" (v. 30).

The details Jesus gives—and does not give—here are not incidental. First, the victim was not on just any road but the well-known, treacherous, seventeen-mile, windy road from Jerusalem, the religious center, to Jericho, located on the west edge of the desert. It was a road known for its danger because of thieves and robbers.

Second, the man's ethnic origin is not immediately identifiable. There were two ways to ascertain immediately the ethnic background of an individual who was traveling. One was by their regional accent or language; those were automatic giveaways. But an even more immediate way was by their ethnic, national or religious garb. Each group had a distinctive dress.

What does Jesus tell us about the victim's ethnicity? He is "half dead," which is a precise way of saying that he is unconscious—and therefore unable to speak. And he is stripped naked by the robbers—which means there is no way to peg his origin based on his clothing. Basically, Jesus is saying, "A valuable, nameless human being is in desperate need on the side of the road."

Scene two: The priest. The first possible mercy-giver is the priest: "A priest happened to be going down the same road, and when he saw the man, he passed by on the other side" (v. 31).

We can assume that the priest, being upper-class, is riding a donkey, as the Samaritan will be later in the story. But the priest has a problem. Is the "half dead" man a Jewish neighbor? He can't tell. Even worse, he doesn't know whether the man is dead or alive. A priest was restricted from touching or even coming within six feet of a dead body; doing so would make him ritually unclean. And if he were unclean, he could not fulfill his duties of collecting, distributing and eating the tithes given for sacrifices—which meant he could not feed his family. Moreoever, unclean priests were publicly shamed near the place of worship. So the priest moves to the other side of the road and passes the man by.

The priest held to the belief that the

laws of ritual purity were an end in themselves—not just a means to an end. So he didn't have to think; clearly, the best way to avoid sin was to keep the law. The commandments about defilement were unconditional, whereas the command to "love thy neighbor" was conditional. This being the case, the legal formula said to follow the unconditional law—so compassion became less important.

Scene three: The Levite. After the priest comes a Levite. Levites were responsible for the physical upkeep of the temple and therefore were not on as high a level as the priests. An off-duty Levite, in particular, was not nearly as bound by the law. Yet the end result is the same as with the priest: "So too, a Levite, when he came to the place and saw him, passed by on the other side" (v. 32).

Since the road to Jericho was notoriously dangerous, it was important to know who else was traveling ahead of you. The story therefore assumes that the Levite knows that the priest—his superior—is on the road ahead of him, and that he has already passed by the man. He probably thought, *Why should I do what the priest would not?*

Perhaps the attitude of the priest and the Levite was like that of Lucy in one *Peanuts* comic strip. Charlie Brown asks her, "What is the first thing you think of when you hear that a friend has gone into the hospital?" Lucy's characteristic response is, "I'm glad it wasn't me." The priest and the Levite move to the other side of the road to avoid contact with human need. We too have avenues that serve as "the other side of the road" today. For example, our freeway systems are such that we don't have to come into contact with struggling humanity unless we build it intentionally into our lives. And inside our homes, we can change the channel on TV when an emaciated starving child interrupts our sitcom. We don't want to have our life disrupted.

Scene four: The good Samaritan. Then the hero enters the story: "But a Samaritan, as he traveled, came where the man was; and when he saw him, he took pity on him" (v. 33).

A Samaritan! A hated Samaritan! There was long-standing animosity between Jews and Samaritans dating back to the eighth century B.C. The Samaritans were considered half-breeds because they had mixed their blood with the conquering Assyrians. There was a saying among the Jews that "eating the bread of Samaritans is like eating the flesh of swine." The best way to capture the jarring interjection of this unlikely hero into Jesus' parable is to imagine telling West Bank Palestinians today a story about a "good Jew," or telling Jews in Israel today the story of a "good Palestinian." If Jesus were to tell this story in the United States today he might have chosen a "good Muslim" or maybe, God forbid, a "good homosexual." Jesus' hearers had cut their teeth on hatred toward the Samaritans—and now Jesus is using one as an example of the embodiment of righteousness.

He's also a model of compassion. Note that the phrase used here to describe the Samaritan's response to the half-dead victim is the same as the one used in Luke 15 to describe the father's reaction to the returning prodigal: "when he saw him, he had compassion." (More on this in chapter twelve.)

That compassion is quickly translated into action: "He went to him and bandaged his wounds, pouring on oil and wine" (v. 34). There is an intentional reversal of the order of healing events here. Typically you would clean the wound with oil first, then disinfect it with wine and *then* bind it. But Jesus places the binding of the wounds first to highlight the true function of the oil and wine in the parable. Both were elements of worship for the Jews; pouring wine and oil was part of making a sacrifice. Thus the real priest in this story, the Samaritan, offers true worship by pouring out the elements of worship on the victim—the same elements that the priest and Levite would use in their ritual ceremony.

Sometimes acts of compassion can put a person in danger. The Samaritan's next move is to "put the man on his own donkey, took him to an inn and took care of him" (v. 34). Blood feuds and retaliation were and still are a part of Middle Eastern life. If a member of your family is hurt or killed, vengeance is part of family honor. And if you can't find the actual assailant, any member of his family will do. The Samaritan therefore puts himself in peril by associating himself with the victim. It would be much like an Indian carrying a scalped cowboy into Dodge City in 1875. Even after he picks the man up, he could have kept his identity hidden by just dropping the man off at a nearby inn, but he stays and takes care of him, ensuring that the victim's family would find out who he is.

The Samaritan doesn't stop there, though. He goes ahead and pays upfront for the man's care: "The next day he took out two silver coins and gave them to the innkeeper. 'Look after him,' he said, 'and when I return, I will reimburse you for any extra expense you may have'" (v. 35). In all this, then, the Samaritan freely demonstrates unexpected love, despite the time, effort, money and personal danger it cost him.

JESUS IS THE SAMARITAN

Why does Jesus choose a Samaritan as the hero of the story? The next logical progression from the priest and Levite would be a Jewish layman with responsibilities in the temple. Through the Samaritan, though, I believe Jesus is giving us a portrait of himself and the work he came to do. He, in fact, *is* the hated Samaritan. The Jews had actually taunted him about this, asking, "Aren't we right in saying that you are a Samaritan and demon-possessed?" (John 8:48). Jesus comes from outside and is not constrained by the laws of the Jews that separated people. Rather, he violates convention if it gets in the way of loving people. Moreoever, the pouring out of the wine and oil is similar to Jesus pouring out his life on the cross as a substitute for our sin. Binding the wounds of the victim conjures up the prophecy from Isaiah 53:5: "But he was pierced for our transgressions, he was crushed for our iniquities; the punishment that brought us peace was upon him, and by his wounds we are healed." As the Samaritan was willing to become the object of a blood-feud for the sake of this unnamed but valued human, so Jesus poured out his blood for us. And as the Samaritan paid the expenses for the wholeness of the victim, so Jesus made the ultimate payment with his life on our behalf.

This story, then, cannot be turned into just a nice moral—"be good to those in need"—that is separated from Jesus. For Jesus is the embodiment of mercy.

Having finished the parable, Jesus is now ready to respond to the lawyer's challenge, "Who is my neighbor?" Cutting through the smokescreen of the law, he asks the lawyer a question that a kindergartner could not miss: "Which of these three do you think was a neighbor to the man who fell into the hands of robbers?" (v. 36). The entangled morass of the law looks foolish in the light of this story. What could the lawyer say but the obvious? "The one who had mercy on him" (v. 37). The very thing for which the lawyer had demonstrated no comprehension he now finally acknowledges.

Jesus again will allow no speculative dialogue. "Go and do likewise," he says. Jesus is not telling the lawyer to go out and justify himself before God by inwardly conjuring up mercy that he does not have. Rather, the command is meant to drive the lawyer to ask, "Then who can be saved?" He, like us, must first see himself as that helpless victim on the side of the road in need of a Savior—as one for whom

the Samaritan Christ lays down his life. Only then, when we know ourselves to be helpless, can we find that we are not worthless. Indeed, only then can we know our worth. For eternal life and salvation are never the result of our efforts to attain them but come to us as a gift from the hated Samaritan Christ, who comes unexpectedly from the outside and takes care of it all. The precondition to give mercy, then, is the knowledge that we ourselves need mercy.

Our hearts naturally turn to the question Jesus posed at the conclusion of this parable. Dallas Willard summarizes the challenge:

> Jesus deftly rejects the question "Who is my neighbor?" and substitutes the only question really relevant here: "To whom will I be a neighbor?" And he knows that we can only answer this question case by case as we go through our days. In the morning we cannot yet know who our neighbor will be that day. The condition of our heart will determine who along our path turns out to be our neighbor, and our faith in God will largely determine whom we have strength enough to make our neighbor.[3]

We follow the Samaritan Christ. He is the ultimate outsider who has come to rescue us who are along the side of the road, without regard for any evaluative human distinctions that we might place on others to justify keeping our distance. The question remains, Will we—we who have encountered and been rescued by a Christ who risked his life—be the kind of people who have a merciful and compassionate heart in the face of human suffering?

---

[1]In my explication of this parable I am leaning heavily on the work and insights of Kenneth Bailey in his book *Jesus Through Middle Eastern Eyes: Cultural Studies in the Gospels* (Downers Grove, Ill.: IVP Academic, 2008).

[2]Thomas Walter Manson, *The Sayings of Jesus* (Grand Rapids: Eerdmans, 1979), p. 61.

[3]Dallas Willard, *The Divine Conspiracy* (San Francisco: HarperCollins, 1998), p. 111.

Reading Study Guide

1. What is problematic about reducing the message of the parable of the good Samaritan and that of Christianity in general to a set of moral principles?

2. How would you describe the mindset of the lawyer who approached Jesus?

3. What was Jesus' approach to handling the lawyer's inquiry?

   Why did Jesus refuse to answer his questions?

4. What was the intent behind the lawyer's question "Who is my neighbor?"

5. What do we know about the victim in the story, and why are the details important?

6. Selecting the religious leaders (a priest and a Levite) as the villains in the story was deliberate. Why do you think Jesus chose them?

7. Jesus scandalizes his listeners by choosing a hated Samaritan as the hero in the story. Why?

Honestly assess your attitude toward various groups of people. Because of your past experience or present mindset, who would you have a very difficult time loving or even wanting God to bless?

8. How is the Samaritan like Jesus?

9. We are being called to take on a heart of mercy and compassion toward the helpless without discrimination and with a willingness to give time and money to meet the needs of others. What place does broken humanity have in your current expression of your faith?

Going Deeper

Stearns, Richard. *The Hole in Our Gospel.* Nashville: Thomas Nelson, 2010. I have read no better challenge to the Christian church. Stearns calls us to complete our understanding of the gospel through the dimension of caring for the least of these on a worldwide scale. He also presents the good news: the church of Jesus Christ could greatly relieve the world's suffering if it was serious about its mission.

11 / Love Those Who Would Do You Harm

LOOKING AHEAD

MEMORY VERSES: Romans 12:20-21
BIBLE STUDY: 1 Corinthians 6:1-8
READING: Overcome Evil with Good

 Core Truth

If we are to have mercy without restriction on any neighbor who is in need, what is our obligation to those who intend our harm?

Jesus raises the stakes even higher when he says, "Love your enemies, do good to those who hate you" (Luke 6:27). In matters of personal injury we are called to forgive and even absorb injustice. In matters requiring the redress of social injustice, Jesus calls us to non-violent, loving resistance to the forces of evil.

1. Identify key words or phrases in the question and answer above, and state their meaning in your own words.

2. Restate the core truth in your own words.

3. What questions or issues does the core truth raise for you?

Memory Verse Study Guide

In the first eleven chapters of his letter to the Romans, Paul scopes out God's master plan of salvation. Chapter 12 then marks a turning point, where Paul begins to spell out the implications for how we are to live—especially in our personal relationships—in light of the mercy of God. In Romans 12:14, 17-19, Paul describes the way of love with special focus on loving those who intend our harm. Note the consistent echo of Jesus' call to not respond in kind but to "overcome evil with good."

1. *Putting it in context:* Read Romans 12:9-19. How does Paul exhort us to live in general, as well as in particular with those who do not have our best interests at heart?

2. The memory verses are *Romans 12:20-21.* Copy the verses verbatim.

3. Quoting Proverbs 25:21-22, Paul gives very specific guidance as to how to treat our enemies. What is it?

4. The intended outcome of these actions is that "in doing this, you will heap burning coals on his head." Do some research to understand this idiom. What will doing good to those who are our enemies potentially bring upon them?

5. Paul lays out the principle of not simply giving back to someone the same thing you have received. What would most likely happen if you did simply respond to others in kind?

6. Think of a situation in your own life in the past or currently where the response could have been or should be to "overcome evil with good." What comes to mind? Is there some action you are convicted to take?

Inductive Bible Study Guide

Sometimes the best Bible studies are those that force us to apply in a very specific way the hard teachings of our Lord. Paul provides us with such a case study. In 1 Corinthians 6 he addresses the disputes that had arisen among the believers and led to lawsuits before the secular courts. He considers this shameful and urges them to settle matters internally and even allow themselves to be wronged. This text appears to be a very specific application of Jesus' teaching to love those who seek our harm and then bear the injustice.

1. *Read 1 Corinthians 6:1-8*. What behavior is so upsetting to Paul?

2. What suggestion does Paul give for how fellow believers should settle disputes they have with each other?

3. What (if any) similar situations between believers within your own church community are you aware of (e.g., tense business transactions, marriage difficulties, disagreements of various kinds, etc.)?

   How might Paul's suggestion for how to resolve these matters be carried out in the church?

4. Ultimately Paul says that these disputes should have never gotten this far, because believers should be willing to be cheated or wronged. Give your honest response to Paul's admonition.

5. Describe a situation where you were treated unjustly. What were the feelings associated with the situation? How did you handle it?

If you had the opportunity to handle that situation again in light of this chapter, how might you respond differently?

⟨👓⟩ Reading: Overcome Evil with Good

This chapter raises the next logical question: how far are we to stretch the definition of neighbor? Through the parable of the good Samaritan, Jesus has already stated that our neighbor is any human being—without qualification—in need of mercy. Isn't that enough? No. Jesus goes beyond this, calling us to also love even those who desire our harm.

In the discipleship manual of the New Testament that we have come to know as the Sermon on the Mount, Jesus astoundingly calls those of us who dare to be his followers to "love [our] enemies and pray for those who persecute [us]" (Matthew 5:44) or, as Luke adds, "do good to those who hate [us]" (Luke 6:27). Why? Because we are to be different. Anyone can love those who love them or lend to those who will pay them back. Followers of Jesus, though, will reflect the heart of his Father. And we have a Father who puts no limits on his love; he shines the sun and sends the rain on the just and unjust alike, for to be "perfect" (Matthew 5:48) is to "be merciful, just as your Father is merciful" (Luke 6:36). The bar has been raised as high as it can be.

I should say from the outset that these texts are some of the most revered and reviled in Jesus' teaching. They are *revered* because they lay out a sacrificial ideal in the face of evil that seems so heroic that few have aspired to keep them. They are *reviled,* on the other hand, be-

cause the message seems hopelessly idealistic and naive. Some would argue that what Jesus is asking us to do would never work in the real world because the only message that the evil forces understand is greater counterforce.

But if we look more closely, we will find contained here in the starkest terms the lifestyle of the cross as modeled by our crucified Lord. If we truly want to know how closely we're following the way of the cross, we must look at how we respond to those who intend our harm and inflict injustice. These texts—and our obedience to them—are the benchmark as to whether we are serious about being followers of the wounded Lamb of God. In this chapter we'll focus particularly on Jesus' words in Matthew 5:38-42, in part because of the specificity of the action that Jesus lays out and because of how often this passage is misunderstood and misapplied.

DO NOT RESIST AN EVIL PERSON?
The key to unlocking the meaning of this text is the befuddling command "Do not resist an evil person" (Matthew 5:39). At first glance, this sounds absurd. Do not oppose an evil person? How could Jesus possibly be teaching that? In fact, it seems contrary to everything he stood for and lived out. How could Jesus be telling his followers to do the opposite of what he himself did? Jesus was not Messiah Milquetoast or the Divine Doormat. He exposed

the evil that resides in the human heart. He berated the scribes and Pharisees in graphic terms, calling them "whitewashed tombs, . . . full of dead men's bones" (Matthew 23:27). And you don't, after all, crucify people who simply roll over in silence before the powers that be. You only put people to death because they are a threat. Clearly, we must be missing something.

Putting the phrase in its context helps us discern what it means, as do Jesus' three word pictures that illustrate it: turning the other cheek, giving up your cloak and going the extra mile.

The law of just retribution. First, Jesus contrasts his radical call to not resist an evildoer with the prevailing view of justice: "You have heard that it was said, 'Eye for eye, and tooth for tooth'" (Matthew 5:38). This law, one of the oldest in civilization, was known as the *lex talionis,* or the law of just retribution. It was an integral part of the ancient Code of Hammurabi. In Israel's case, the law appears in Exodus, in the section immediately following the Ten Commandments (Exodus 21–23). Here's just one example of the *lex talionis* as recorded in Scripture, in this case regarding men who cause the miscarriage of a pregnant woman while they're fighting: "If there is serious injury, you are to take life for life, eye for eye, tooth for tooth, hand for hand, foot for foot, burn for burn, wound for wound, bruise for bruise" (Exodus 21:23-25).

As brutal as it might sound, we must recognize that the implementation of the law of just retribution was actually a great advance in a tribal society. First, it limited revenge in a society where revenge escalated rapidly and went far beyond the original offense. The pattern was not unlike Buck's description of a feud in Mark Twain's classic *Adventures of Huckleberry Finn:* "Well a feud is this way: A man has a quarrel with another man, and kills him; then that other man's brother kills him; then the other brothers on both sides, goes for one another; then the cousins chip in—by and by everybody's killed off, and there ain't no more feud. But it's kind of slow and takes a long time."[1] This was what this law was intended to stop.

Second, the law moved punishment out of the arena of personal revenge and into the courts with the rule of law so that a judge would determine the equivalency of "eye for eye, and tooth for tooth." The punishment was therefore more likely to fit the crime, administered as it was by the court and not by the parties personally involved. The law of just retribution was thus a great step forward in controlling the lawlessness of the day.

Against this backdrop, then, let's attempt to unlock the meaning of this troublesome command, "Do not resist an evil person." A careful look at the original words themselves helps, and the illustrations Jesus gives us add further application.

The phrase "do not resist" used here is taken from a compound word in the Greek language, *anti-stenai. Anti* means "against," and *stenai* in noun form refers to "a violent or armed rebellion, insurrection or riot." So a better translation would be, "Do not violently resist an evil person." "Do not strike back in kind." "Don't give blow for blow." This makes much more sense in the context; Jesus is saying that even though the law of retributive justice was a great advance, we are to live out the law of love for our neighbor, which includes our enemies. The meaning here is that we are not to use the same means or adopt the ways of those who would deploy force or demeaning behavior in order to harm us.

So the real issue here is not *whether* we resist evil but *how*. The world only knows two ways to deal with the oppressive evil or injustice of the powerful. The first is *passivity* (flight): "Roll over and allow yourself to be exploited. It is too costly to fight back. Just take it." Some would say Jesus' command is an encouragement to us to respond this way—to use the rope-a-dope method of fighting deployed by Muhammad Ali on occasion, which is basically letting your opponent punch himself out; offer no resistance, and eventually the oppressor will get tired or evil will run its course.

The second way of the world is to *violently resist* (fight): "You must fight fire with fire. The only language a bully understands is you punching back harder than you were punched." Whether in a school hallway or in the foreign policy of nations, this is the predominant attitude that has been adopted.

Jesus offers a third way. He calls us to a lifestyle of nonviolent, loving resistance to evil or injustice that refuses to adapt or sink to the level of the evildoer.

The best way to understand Jesus' command here is through the illustrations that he gives. Each of the three illustrations paints a picture of a powerless, oppressed, exploited person responding in a nonviolent, loving way to his oppressor—a way that allows the victim to gain control while affirming the dignity and worth of the perpetrator and providing them with an opportunity for redemption. Let's look at each of Jesus' illustrations.

1. Turn the other cheek. "If someone strikes you on the right cheek," Jesus says in his first example, "turn to him the other also" (Matthew 5:39). It may sound to our ears like Jesus is saying, "If someone punches you on the right cheek, turn the left cheek toward him and invite him to punch you there as well." But again, this is not at first glance what it appears; it isn't actually about a fist fight. Jesus is not advocating that we allow someone to pummel us into the ground. What, then, is envisioned here? If you were standing face to face with a right-handed person and they were to strike you on the right cheek, how would they do it? They would have to reach out with the back of their hand. In Jewish society this was not so much an act of physical violence but an insult meant to demean, humiliate or degrade. In other words, it was a case of a more powerful person putting a lesser person in their place.

The advice given by Jesus to turn the other cheek is therefore intended to put the victim of this humiliation in control. A way to take charge of the situation, rather than just slink off in silence, was to actively present the other cheek as well. By taking the initiative the victim would show that the blow did not have the intended effect. It was like saying, "Try again. I deny you the right to humiliate me. You may try, but I don't feel the same way about myself as you do." In addition, actively presenting the other cheek was a way of exposing the shame of the oppressor's deed, and revealing them for what they were: a person who degrades another. In this sense, it gave evildoers the opportunity to see themselves as they were and to be redeemed from it.

2. Give your cloak. For his next example Jesus says, "If someone wants to sue you and take your tunic, let him have your cloak as well" (Matthew 5:40). Given the cultural gap between the twenty-first-century world and Jesus' day, we're not likely to immediately comprehend the absurd picture that Jesus is painting. The scenario would have taken place in a courtroom, with a wealthy person attempting to collect on a debt owed. So callous is the oppressor in Jesus' illustration that he wants to take the last thing the debtor has: his clothes. There are two pieces of clothing mentioned here. The tunic, the item that the wealthy person is demanding, is a long sacklike undergarment, whereas the cloak is a blanketlike outer garment used by the poor to protect themselves against the weather. The Old Testament law—which provided protection for the poor against exploitation by the rich and powerful—

said explicitly that if a rich person took the cloak (the outer garment) as collateral to secure a loan, it had to be returned by sundown (Exodus 22:25-27).

Jesus, frankly, is employing some cheeky humor here. His advice to the sued party is to not only give his underwear, but also his outerwear, so that he would be standing there naked in court. This brings to my mind the attire of Mahatma Gandhi, who applied Jesus' teaching of nonviolent resistance as he fought for India's independence against the almighty British Empire. Gandhi met with royalty, dressed in their regal garb and surrounded by luxury, wrapped only in a *dhoti,* the simplest attire of the powerless. The contrast could not have been more dramatic.

Again, Jesus is implying here that the way to gain control and reveal the dishonor of the powerful is to go beyond even the shameful thing that is being asked. This is like sentencing a slumlord to live in his own dilapidated buildings. In so doing, the powerful must experience the life that they are forcing on others. It gives the one who is exploiting others a chance to see life from the degraded one's perspective. This also provides a context for someone to see what they have become and then change.

3. Go the extra mile. As his last illustration, Jesus instructs, "If someone forces you to go one mile, go with him two miles" (Matthew 5:41). The setting for Jesus' admonition would have been very clear to his listeners: the occupying Roman army would conscript Israelis to carry their sixty-five to eighty-five-pound packs for a prescribed distance. Indeed, the first-century Jewish historian Josephus used the word *force* specifically to mean the compulsory transportation of military baggage. Yet, the Romans were sensitive about inciting the anger of the oppressed, so Roman soldiers were instructed to only compel someone to carry their equipment for a limited distance. There were even "mile-markers" so that the soldiers would not overstep their bounds.

How, then, were the conscripted to take initiative and preserve their dignity? By saying cheerfully to the Roman soldier when they reached the mile-marker, "Please, I'm not done. Let me carry your pack another mile." In so doing, the oppressed one gains the control, because they now make it their decision to aid the soldier. This creates a quandary for the oppressor; the soldier would most likely say to himself, "Why is this person doing this? Why are they being so kind to me?" The impact made is consistent with the idiom Paul uses when he says that, in giving food and drink to our enemies, we *"heap burning coals on his head"* (Romans 12:20). Today we have the expression "Kill 'em with kindness."

These three illustrations give us a picture of what it means to "not resist violently an evil person." Jesus urges his followers to adopt the lifestyle of nonviolent, loving resistance to oppressive evil and injustice in order to establish the value of even our enemies.

FORESHADOWING OF THE CROSS

Each of these illustrations is also a foreshadowing of the most creative redemptive act ever performed, the cross of Jesus. On the cross, the Lord of glory submitted to humiliating injustice, thereby exposing the evil of the human heart.

After his trial and before his crucifixion, the Roman soldiers had some time to kill, so they decided to make sport of the One we love. Draping a purple cape of royalty across his bloodied and raw shoulders and placing in his hand a reed for a scepter, they made fun of the "King of the Jews." They even twisted thorny branches into a crown, which pierced his scalp. In mock honor they then bowed before the caricature of their making, egging each other on with laughter. All of this precedes the horror of the cross, which I will refrain from describing because the evil one devised a method of barbarous torture so hideous as to be unspeakable.

Jesus willingly submitted to this degradation even though he could have ended it at any moment. I believe one of the reasons for his submission was so that we could graphically see the evil we are all capable of. Henri Nouwen illustrates the power of the cross to expose the evil of the human heart through a tragic story of a family in Paraguay. The father, a doctor, was outspoken against the human-rights abuses of the military government. The local police took revenge by arresting his son and hideously torturing him to death. Enraged townsfolk wanted to turn the boy's funeral into a protest march, but the father had an idea that was the way of Jesus. At the funeral, the father displayed his son's body as he found it in jail—naked, scarred from electric shocks and cigarette burnings and beatings. All the villagers filed past the son's corpse, which lay not in a coffin but on the blood-soaked mattress from the prison.[2] It put injustice on public display like nothing else could. This is what the cross does. It exposes the capacity of the human heart for evil.

Yet the cross is also designed to provide the redemptive possibility. The thieves crucified on either side of Jesus were most likely cursing their executioners. Reports say that a person undergoing the excruciating pain of having nails driven through the nerve endings of their extremities wailed like a wounded animal in the wilderness. But what do we hear from the mouth of Jesus? "Father, forgive them, for they do not know what they are doing" (Luke 23:34). Jesus would not get even. He did not say, "Just wait. My Father will get you for this one day." Rather, Jesus dramatically portrays the mercy of God on the cross. This is why he can say to us, "Be merciful, just as your Father is merciful" (Luke 6:36).

The new life in the kingdom of God is the loving way of the cross. When we are offended, mistreated, unjustly accused, caricatured or maligned, we are to remember the One we follow. At these moments we must go back to the foot of the cross and hear the words of Jesus to us, "Father, forgive them, for they do not know what they are doing." And, by reminding ourselves that we helped put Jesus there through our own sin, we can borrow the grace and power of our crucified Lord and offer creative love to those who would seek our harm.

WHY THE WAY OF THE CROSS?

In addition to being obedient to the model of our Lord, why should we choose the way of the cross and love our enemies? Five compelling reasons come to mind.

First, it is the only possible way to *break the cycle of violence and retribution*. Hate begets hate. Vilification begets vilification. When we hold on to our pain as the injured party, we see our "opponent" only through the lens of our hurt and thus continue to replay the video of injustice. The only way to extricate our self and get off the so-called hamster wheel of anger and bitterness is to forgive. Episcopal priest Gale Webbe has written, "The only ultimate way to conquer evil is to let it be smothered within a willing, living, human being. When it is absorbed there, like blood in a sponge, it loses its power and goes no further."[3]

Second, it provides the possibility of *redemption of the opponent*. Though I previously mentioned this, it is worth underscoring. The hope is to turn the enemy into a brother or sister. And, toward this end, the Christian life is about invincible good will: No matter what anyone does to me, I will never seek to do harm to another; I will never set out for revenge; I will always seek nothing but the highest good.

Third, by choosing the loving way of the

cross we *refuse to become like our ene-mies.* If you use the means of your enemy you will inevitably succumb to hate and become like the one oppressing you. African American leader and orator Booker T. Washington, who was born into slavery, said, "Let no man pull you so low as to make you hate him."[4]

Fourth, loving our enemies reminds us that *the universe is on the side of justice.* When the apostle Paul expounds on this theme of Jesus' in Romans 12, he writes, "Do not repay anyone evil for evil. . . . Do not take revenge, my friends, but leave room for God's wrath, for it is written: 'It is mine to avenge; I will repay'" (Romans 12:17, 19). Admittedly, we may not see in time the justice we desire; we might have to wait for eternity for the balance sheet of God to be executed. But we're also reminded here that we rarely see things exactly as they are; rather, we see through the distorted lens of our experience. Only God can take it all into account. We're to let God do the sorting.

Finally, one of the greatest motivations toward having a generosity of spirit is that *it is the freest way to live.* A liberated person is one who remains in control, refusing to allow the offense of another to determine how they will respond. In these situations, we are essentially saying to those who do not wish us well, "You will not determine the terms of engagement. I refuse to return evil for evil. It makes no difference what you do; I will still have a choice about how I respond, and my choice is to love you."

STORIES OF UNCONQUERABLE LOVE

To close this chapter on this most demanding way of love, let me give two powerful illustrations of the embodiment of these five principles. The first is the story of remarkable forgiveness on a personal level. The second story applies these principles of nonviolence and love at a social level to fight vile injustice.

A model for personal forgiveness. The first story is that of Jennifer Thompson-Cannino and Ron Cotton as told in their book, *Picking Cotton.* As a twenty-two-year-old college student, Jennifer was brutally raped at knifepoint in her apartment. "I hated this man with a vengeance and a blind hate that I can't even articulate," she later wrote. She also remembered him clearly; during the attack she had somehow had the presence of mind to pay attention to the facial features of her attacker. With her attacker's visage firmly fixed in her mind, then, she picked Ron Cotton out of both a photo book and a police lineup. Ron stood trial, was found guilty and was sentenced to life plus fifty years in prison. Two years later, Jennifer went through the agony of another trial because the appellate court had overturned the original decision. This time Ron was found guilty of not one but two rapes, and condemned to two life sentences plus fifty-four years. And Jennifer celebrated. "This bad guy was going to prison forever," she wrote, "never ever to be free again, never to find love, never to have children."

Then the unthinkable happened. A DNA

test proved that Ron Cotton was not Jennifer's attacker. Another man, already in prison for other offenses, was the guilty party. At this point Ron had spent four thousand days—eleven years—in prison. Jennifer was sick that she could have been so wrong, and that she had perpetrated this kind of hell on another. It took her two years after Ron's release to work up the nerve to ask for his forgiveness.

A meeting was arranged in a pastor's study, where the two faced each other for the first time outside of a police lineup or a courtroom. Jennifer trembled with emotion. She said to Ron, "Mr. Cotton. I don't even know what to call you. Ron? Ronald? Mr. Cotton? If I spent the rest of my life telling you how sorry I am, it wouldn't come close to how I feel. Can you forgive me?"

Ron had learned to read people's faces; he knew that people talk with their eyes. And he knew that she was truly sorry for the unbelievable pain her false testimony had inflicted on his life. "If she could have gone back in time and turned the hands of time to change what happened," Ron wrote, "she would have." He said to her, "I forgive you. I'm not angry at you. I don't want you to spend the rest of your life looking over your shoulder, thinking I'm out to get you, or harm your family. If you look, I'm not going to be there. All I want is for us all to go on and have a happy life."

Ron recalls this moment in their book: "Jennifer looked at me speechless. Her whole face trembled and she got tears in her brown eyes. I could see there was pain,

a lot of pain that she was trying to let go. For the first time, in so many years, I didn't see the hate in her eyes. She didn't look at me and see the man who had hurt her, the man she wanted dead, she saw me. I didn't even think about it until after the fact, but I reached for her hands and all of a sudden, we were standing there hugging."

Forgiveness in the face of life's horrible injustices gives life back to both victim and perpetrator. Today Ron and Jennifer and their families are dear friends. They regularly appear together to tell their story of forgiveness and speak on behalf of those who may be wrongly convicted.[5]

Martin Luther King Jr.: A model of nonviolent, loving resistance. The second story comes from the life of a man who embodied the teaching and spirit of Jesus to take on the evil of racial discrimination. The legacy of slavery in the United States created a social structure where black people were treated as lower-level human beings who were to serve their powerful white oppressors. But in the 1950s, a voice came from the church of Jesus Christ to declare that this injustice would not stand. Martin Luther King Jr., through the influence of his father, also a pastor, had refused to see himself in the denigrating perspective perpetuated by those who expected a black person to take a lower station in life. Through his studies in college and seminary and in his doctoral work, King had formulated an approach to combating this injustice that was rooted in Jesus' teaching in the Sermon on the Mount. He described it this way: "Christ furnished the spirit and motivation while Gandhi furnished the method."[6]

King built his entire approach to confronting structural racial discrimination and the perpetrators of it on the philosophy of nonviolent, loving resistance. His philosophy had nothing to do with simply absorbing and accepting the evil action of racism, but rather deploying methods and strategies that would confront the injustices, but always in a nonviolent, loving way. King said that his approach was intended to not only elevate the dignity of the black person but also liberate the white oppressors who were demeaning themselves as well by their actions. In other words, the goal was not simply to elevate his people but also to create a "loving community."

Anyone who joined King's movement had to be committed to living out non-retaliatory, loving responses and had to go through training so that they could handle anything thrown at them. So whether it was integrating a bus in Montgomery, Alabama; marching for voting rights in Selma, Alabama; standing with underpaid and exploited sanitation workers in Memphis, Tennessee; integrating a lunch counter in Birmingham, Alabama; or standing for fair housing in Chicago, all violence was to be met with a loving, nonviolent response. Young black college students were pulled from Woolworth's lunch counters and beaten by angry mobs, but they did not return violence for violence. Powerful water hoses sent people skidding along pavement; growling, vicious dogs bared their frightening teeth; and police on horseback swung belly clubs at defenseless crowds, but the people simply took it, as the nation watched in horror at what racism was capable of.

Even when other actors in the civil rights movement were advocating violence, Martin Luther King, to the day he was assassinated on April 4, 1968, never wavered from his conviction that the way of Jesus was the third way—the way of the kingdom of God.

This is a lifestyle we can never live in our own strength. To have mercy we must receive mercy. In other words, we must see our need for mercy before we can live in it. So we must first find mercy in the cross. Then, whether we are dealing with the pain of personal injustice or standing with those who are the victims of the powerful, we will be able to love even our enemies, and so follow the way of Jesus.

---

[1]Mark Twain, *The Adventures of Huckleberry Finn* (Charleston, S.C.: BookSurge Classics, 2004), p. 107.

[2]Retold in Philip Yancey, *Disappointment with God* (Grand Rapids: Zondervan, 1988), p. 185.

[3]Gale D. Webbe, quoted in ibid., p. 129.

[4]Booker T. Washington, *Up from Slavery: An Autobiography of Booker T. Washington* (Charleston, S.C.: CreateSpace, 2009), chap. 11.

[5]Jennifer Thompson-Cannino and Ronald Cotton with Erin Torneo, *Picking Cotton: Our Memoir of Injustice and Redemption* (New York: St. Martin's Press, 2009).

[6]Martin Luther King Jr., *The Autobiography of Martin Luther King, Jr.,* ed. Clayborne Carson (New York: Grand Central, 1998), p. 67.

Reading Study Guide

1. What is your honest reaction to Jesus' expectation that his followers love their enemies? Is this more than human beings should be asked to do? Why or Why not?

2. This article asserts that there are three ways that we can deal with evil's intention. Describe each:

   a. Passivity (flight):

   b. Violent resistance (fight):

   c. Nonviolent, loving resistance:

3. How do you react to the accusation that Jesus' third way is hopelessly idealistic and naive.

4. Explain how each of the three word pictures Jesus paints illustrates his principle of nonviolent, loving resistance to evil.

   a. "Turn the other cheek":

   b. "Give your cloak":

   c. "Go the extra mile":

5. How is the cross foreshadowed in these images?

6. The reading lists five reasons why we should choose the way of the cross. Which of these is most compelling to you? Why?

7. Very few of us will go through life without some sort of personal pain that will put us in the position of needing to forgive someone else. How does the story of Ron Cotton and Jennifer Thompson-Cannino speak to you?

8. How might we apply the philosophy of nonviolent, loving resistance employed by Martin Luther King Jr. to evil in our day?

Is there an issue of injustice on your heart that this approach could be used to fight?

Going Deeper

King Jr., Martin Luther. *The Autobiography of Martin Luther King, Jr.* Edited by Clayborne Carson. New York: Grand Central, 1998. One of the messages that consistently runs through the entirety of King's philosophy and life is a commitment to Jesus' call to nonviolent, loving resistance to injustice, in order to redeem both the oppressed and oppressor to form a loving community.

12 / Demonstrate Compassion: Love's Evidence

LOOKING AHEAD

MEMORY VERSES: 1 John 3:16-18
BIBLE STUDY: James 2:14-26
READING: Compassion: Sympathy and Outrage

 Core Truth

How do we demonstrate our love for God?

Jesus has made our love for our neighbor inseparable from our love for God. We cannot say that we love God if we don't love our neighbor. Thus, the evidence that we do love God is the observable demonstration of compassion. Compassion combines merciful identification with the needs of our neighbor with outrage against the forces of injustice that have degraded the quality of a human life.

1. Identify key words or phrases in the question and answer above, and state their meaning in your own words.

2. Restate the core truth in your own words.

3. What questions or issues does the core truth raise for you?

Memory Verse Study Guide

The apostle John makes it unequivocally clear that there is an unbreakable link between our love for God and our love for our brothers and sisters in Christ. The context of John's remarks for our memory verses appears to be the family of God; Scripture states that the first obligation of love is to those of the household of faith. Jesus said to his disciples, "By this all men will know that you are my disciples, if you love one another" (John 13:35).

1. *Putting it in context:* Read 1 John 3:11-24. In what terms does John establish the link between our love for God and our love for the family of God?

2. The memory verses are *1 John 3:16-18*. Copy the verses verbatim.

3. John tells us that the model of our love for the family of God is Jesus. What model did Jesus establish for how we're to love others (see v. 16)?

4. Our love is to be demonstrated in very practical terms. In verse 17, what specific way are we called to express our love?

5. Share a time when you have had the opportunity to be on either the giving end or the receiving end of compassion. What was the experience like?

   Is there a current opportunity to love someone within the family of God that you think the Holy Spirit might be bringing to your attention?

6. How would you define what love is according to John?

Inductive Bible Study Guide

James, the brother of Jesus, continues the theme of the inseparability of loving God and loving our neighbor, but on different terms: he links together faith and works. The great Reformer Martin Luther had difficulty with James because of his emphasis on works. It seemed to Luther that James was making works a means of salvation. What James was actually doing, though, was seeing works as a demonstration of salvation. In other words, if faith has no practical outworkings, is there really any faith at all?

1. *Read James 2:14-26.* Summarize James's overall argument regarding the connection between faith and works.

2. Why does James consider the evidence of works vital to proving that faith is real?

3. How does James characterize faith that's not accompanied by works (see v. 17 especially)?

4. What kinds of works does James have in mind? What do his illustrations tell us about what good works look like?

5. What is the overall error that James so stridently attempts to correct?

6. In what ways does this same error manifest itself in the Christian community today?

Reading: Compassion: Sympathy and Outrage

I have a vivid memory from early in my ministry when we were forming small groups through our church among university graduate students. I was leading a group of four or five couples who were relative strangers. It became clear to me in one of our first gatherings that this group was going to be a challenge when one man announced without embarrassment (and I quote): "I hate people." As the group leader, I didn't know what to say after that. All I remember is being stunned.

What Jesus is telling us in the Essential Commandment is that you can't love God without loving people. In other words, you can't have affection for God without having it translate into deep engagement in the welfare of others. And deep engagement does not mean just claiming a warm fuzzy feeling toward humanity; it involves genuine care for the quality of life of specific people.

One word captures the way Jesus interacted with his rebellious creation and the way our hearts should tilt toward the world as well. It is the word *compassion*. And our service to the world is found at the intersection of the compassion of Christ in us and a place of brokenness in people's lives. This reading can help you discover where that place is for you. That answer, in turn, will guide you into your place of service and purpose.

COMPASSION: WHAT IS IT?
We first need to understand the biblical meaning of compassion, especially as it was displayed in the life and heart of Jesus Christ. In the Hebrew understanding of our human makeup, compassion emanates from the depths of one's being; it is associated with the guts or innards—with a clutch in the stomach or a gut reaction. So, in response to a deeply moving story, you might hear a Middle Easterner say, "You are cutting up my intestines." The pronunciation of the Greek word for compassion, *splagnxizomai,* actually reflects this meaning.

Jesus will serve as our model for compassion as we follow him through the Gospels. He demonstrates that compassion is a blend of *sympathy* and *outrage: sympathetic* identification with a person's plight and *outrage* at the external forces that have diminished a person's quality of life.

Sympathy. The writer of Hebrews says of Jesus, "For we do not have a high priest who is unable to *sympathize* with our weaknesses, but we have one who has been tempted in every way, just as we are—yet was without sin" (Hebrews 4:15). The word for sympathy in Greek is *sunpathos,* which, literally translated, is "to feel or to suffer with."

Sympathy was clearly present in the ministry of Jesus. Whether it was observing the crowds or interacting with an individual, Jesus experienced the gut reaction of identification with their lostness. For example, in Matthew 9 we read, "When

[Jesus] saw the crowds, he had *compassion* on them, because they were harassed and helpless, like sheep without a shepherd" (v. 36). Pouring forth from deep inside him was a spontaneous response toward the populace, for he saw a clueless people. They were "harassed and helpless," literally "mangled and cast down": *harassed* in that they were being led astray by religious leaders who were like the blind leading the blind, and *helpless* in that, like lost sheep, they were unable to extricate themselves from danger. There were no shepherds to guide these sheep to green pastures and still waters. But the fellow-feeling of Jesus—his compassion—doesn't stop with feeling; it motivates mission in his name. Because he shared in the suffering of the crowds, he then instituted mission to them, telling his disciples to pray that the Lord of the harvest would send workers into the harvest so that the crowd would have faithful people to follow (see Matthew 9:37).

On another occasion, Luke tells us, "As [Jesus] approached Jerusalem and saw the city, he wept over it" (Luke 19:41). "O Jerusalem, Jerusalem," he cries elsewhere in Luke's Gospel. These were not crocodile tears that welled up in the corners of his eyes and then trickled down his cheek. No, Jesus burst into tears. His body convulsed in soul-sobbing agony over a people who did not know the hour of their visitation from God himself, or even that they were lost.

The father and the prodigal. There is no greater expression of compassion than that of the father for his prodigal son in Jesus' parable recorded in Luke 15. The father would have been deeply wounded by the younger son's demand to have his share of the inheritance before his father's death. Yet, in an act of love, the father cut his son loose to face life on his own, even knowing the pain that awaited him in the far country. When the son had fallen so low that he was competing with the pigs for food to survive, he realized that life was far better back home in his father's house.

But what should the son expect upon his return home? Since the patriarch in the family had been shamed by the son who wished for his father's death, we might expect that the father would put the son in his place when he arrived home by heaping shame on him. Yet here's how Jesus describes the son's homecoming: "But while [the son] was still a long way off, his father saw him and was filled with *compassion* for him" (v. 20). Where was the father when the son returned? Sitting at home ready to lower the boom? No, the father was on the road leading to the village, inspecting it daily, waiting for his son to return. The waiting Father-God is not cloistered in the heavens untouched by human pain. This is the God who comes to where we are.

What did the father see that drew compassion? In an instant he saw the story of his son's life in the far country in his emaciated, gaunt, disheveled, dragging body, in his smelly clothes, in the way his head hung low. And the father's reaction was to enter into and come alongside his son's pain.

To have sympathy is to have a common, endured and shared experience—a fellowship of suffering. It's to be on the same frequency, heart beating next to someone else's heart, and to feel alongside.

Sympathy in action. A story told to me by a friend helps us see the impact human sympathy from a Christian heart can have.[1] Karen was at the airport waiting to pick up her grandson before Christmas. Her attention was arrested by a somewhat wild woman who marched to the ticket counter. She was a human in disarray. Boisterously, she made some mention to the woman behind the counter about being one of the top two swimmers in the world, speaking loudly enough for others to hear. As she continued, it became clear that she was upset over the delay of her flight. Quite demanding, she asked the counter attendant, "Can you watch my bags?" but was told that wasn't allowed. She then wheeled her bags to the back-to-back rows of chairs where two young boys were sitting eating McDonald's French fries. Reaching back toward them, she said to everyone around her, "I like kids," and asked if she could have some fries. By this time those nearby were hiding behind their newspapers, hoping she wouldn't get any closer.

Two security guards had been called to assess the situation and concluded that she was rational. But Karen, watching all of this, heard an inner voice say, "She hasn't taken her meds this morning." She moved closer to the disoriented woman in the now almost-vacated area. Gently and calmly,

Karen asked her, "Have you taken your meds today? I'm wondering because you're acting like you haven't taken your meds."

The woman's demeanor changed instantly. She abandoned her tough persona and became childlike. "No," she replied, "but they're way packed up in my suitcase." Karen had heard she had a four-hour wait, so she urged the woman to open her bag and find them while she went to get a bottle of water.

After the woman had swallowed her pills, Karen asked, "Someone meeting you in Detroit?"

"Sure. My mom."

"Well, then, you really do want to be in good shape when she picks you up, don't you?"

The woman nodded yes. And then she said, "Thank you for taking care of me."

Filled with a wave of compassion, Karen hugged her and said, "That's what we're here for, isn't it?"

"Sure, we're here for one another."

As Karen reflected on this encounter, she wondered why she was drawn to this woman when others were shying away. A gift of mercy, yes. A love for all God's creation, sure. But more. Karen says, "You see, I have met this lady before. She has inhabited territory within me. We share *simpatico,* an understanding, a communal confusion—just hanging on."

A poem reads, "To mourn is to forget yourself for a moment and get lost in someone else's pain and then, to find yourself in the very act of getting lost." This is what Karen experienced, and what Jesus embodied; our act of identification with the brokenness of another is a sign of our love for Christ.

Outrage. Yet compassion is more than sympathy. Biblical compassion has a component of righteous outrage; it is an anger directed toward circumstances that have diminished the quality of a person's life.

The Gospel of Mark records the story of a leper who approached Jesus and begged him for healing. Leprosy, a disease that causes your skin to rot and to lose all sensitivity to pain, has been compared to HIV/AIDS in our time; having it was as bad as it could get in Jesus' day. The lepers, in other words, were the untouchables of the first century, required to dwell alone outside the city. And when they went about, they had to warn others of their polluted presence by wearing torn clothes, having a shaved head, covering their lips and shouting "Unclean! Unclean!" It was therefore very bold on the leper's part to approach Jesus, but he must have seen or known about Jesus' compassionate heart.

First he affirms Jesus' healing power, saying, "If you are willing, you can make me clean" (Mark 1:40). Mark gives us Jesus' response: "Filled with compassion, Jesus reached out his hand and touched the man. 'I am willing,' he said" (v. 41). A pastor friend of mine used to say, "Watch the hands of Jesus." Here we see Jesus touch a leper. Who knows how long it had been since the man had felt the solace of human contact? This is true sympathy from Jesus.

But then Jesus says, "Be clean!" (v. 41).

You can sense the power behind this command issued by Jesus. He unleashes the full force of moral fury against this leprosy that had reduced the man's life to daily horror. Indeed, you can almost hear the agony emerging somewhere deep down within Jesus' guts, crying, "This is not the way it's supposed to be!"

We see Jesus' outrage over death and disease again in John 11, where the familiar story of the death and raising of Lazarus is recorded. Jesus had become a dear and loving friend of Mary, Martha and Lazarus, frequently staying in their home in Bethany, near Jerusalem. A message was sent to Jesus and his disciples one day, though, informing them that Lazarus was near death. By the time Jesus arrived in Bethany, Lazarus had been in the grave four days. Martha, upon hearing that Jesus had finally come, ran to meet him on the outskirts of the village, wondering out loud why Jesus had not come earlier to heal Lazarus before he had died. Mary too approached Jesus in tears over the loss of her brother. We then read in John 11:33, "When Jesus saw her weeping, and the Jews who had come along with her also weeping, he was *deeply moved in spirit and troubled.*" In this context, the Scripture says, "Jesus wept. Then the Jews said, 'See how he loved him!'" (vv. 35-36).

We might think that all Jesus was feeling here was a sense of loss and shared grief with Mary and Martha—nothing besides sympathy. But there is more going on here. In verse 38 we read, "Jesus, *once more deeply moved,* came to the tomb."

The single word translated "deeply moved" here is the same word used to describe a Greek stallion preparing for battle. It paints a picture of a combat-trained horse, rearing back on its hind legs, pawing the air with muscles rippling, ready to enter the contest. A more literal translation would be, "Jesus, snorting in spirit, came to the tomb."

Os Guinness captures the scene like this:

> Entering his Father's world as the Son of God, he found not order, beauty, harmony and fulfillment, but fractured disorder, raw ugliness, complete disarray—everywhere the abortion of God's original plan. Standing at the graveside, he came face to face with death that symbolized and summarized the accumulation of evil, pain, sorrow, suffering, injustice, cruelty and despair. He was outraged by the outrageous abnormality of death.[2]

In other words, everything in Jesus cried, "This is not the way it's supposed to be." As much as we believe that Jesus, in his resurrection, is the victor over death—and he wonderfully is—sin did enter this world, and the result is death.

Thus, when Jesus called out, "Lazarus, come out!" he was hurling himself into the teeth of all the pain, suffering, interruption and sorrow that death represented. His words and actions here show us that there is a redemptive side to anger, and that love and anger are not incompatible. In fact, there is no love without anger toward the forces that corrupt and demean people's lives.

I remember quite clearly the moment I was caught off-guard by my own angry reaction to death. It was the late 1970s, and I was pastoring a small church in Burbank, California. One of our members, Mildred, was a delightful woman nearing eighty years old. She was a true renaissance woman: an attorney (before females populated the profession), an art collector, widely read. And she always seemed to have something interesting and engaging to say about my sermons. One Sunday morning before worship, while I was still at home, the phone rang. Mildred's brother was on the line. He reported to me that Mildred had been found dead in her home and had probably been dead for a couple of days. When I hung up the phone, I shouted something I had better not put in written form here. A geyser of emotion welled up within me, a gut reaction fueled by anger. It caught me by surprise. Where did that come from? I was livid that Mildred had died and in this way. This was not the way it was supposed to be.

So compassion is a blend of sympathy with righteous anger toward the external circumstances that have conspired to diminish a life.

WHERE YOUR COMPASSION INTERSECTS BROKENNESS

Do we truly desire to follow Jesus to those places where he weeps and is moving against the forces of evil that would corrupt lives?

Richard Stearns, the president of World Vision USA, speaks a prophetic word to a comfortable Western church in his book, *The Hole in Our Gospel*. Essentially he calls for us to take on the heart of Jesus as just described. We have lost the ability to step outside of our own self-interest and take on the pain of others, he claims. And we have lost a sense of moral outrage over the masses of broken humanity who scratch a life from hand to mouth. What makes me able to hear his pointed and uncomfortable message is that Stearns had to go through his own "conversion" experience or change of heart to open himself up to the pain in the world at large.

This is, of course, where we need to start. As we discovered in chapter two, there is no transformation without a broken and contrite heart. When we get in touch with our own need for forgiveness and mercy, then we can come alongside both the spiritual and physical destitution that others face. Can you honestly find that place of sympathy and outrage within your own spirit? If not, a hard-knuckle conversation with our Lord is the place to begin.

Then we can return to the question of where the compassion of Christ in us intersects the brokenness of people's lives. For some of us, the pain we've experienced in our own life becomes our invitation to service. Having gone through the pain of a divorce, you can be there for others experiencing the same thing. Having survived the fear of breast cancer, you might come alongside those who have just received the

diagnosis. Janet, a member of a church I previously served, told me that she was called to intervene with suicidal teenagers, because her sister had committed suicide as a teen. Our pain can become a place of ministry. Think about your own life. Where do you find that you identify in sympathy with the hurts of others but also feel disturbed by the forces that destroy people's lives?

As we each explore this question, Richard Stearns offers us some good news. First, there is huge potential for the Christian church in America to radically address the humanitarian needs of the world. In other words, we have the resources to make a mighty impact that could awaken the world to the compassion of Christians and the Lord we follow. Stearns points out that the American church is the wealthiest community of Christians in the history of Christendom; the total income of American churchgoers is about $5.2 trillion.[3] A major problem is that we tithe only 2.58 percent of this. And when we drill it down we see that only about 2 percent of this amount ever leaves the country to assist the poor or accomplish the worldwide evangelistic mission of the church. This is what Stearns calls the 2 percent of the 2 percent. What would happen if we paid our tithe? We would have an extra $168 billion to spend on funding the work of Christ worldwide.

Here is the even better news: $168 billion "could eliminate the most extreme poverty on the planet for more than a billion people." Moreoever, "Universal primary education for children would cost just $6 billion; the cost to bring clean water to most of the world's poor, an estimated $9 billion; and basic health and nutrition for everyone in the world, $13 billion."[4]

When I read the following I came out of my chair with enthusiasm. Imagine Christians giving so generously that the money they gave

- brought an end to world hunger

- solved the clean water crisis

- provided universal access to drugs and medical care for millions suffering from AIDS, malaria and tuberculosis

- virtually eliminated the more than twenty-six thousand deaths of children daily

- guaranteed education for the world's children

- provided a safety net for the world's tens of millions of orphans[5]

Don't you want to be part of this effort?

Of course, there are huge barriers to accomplishing the above list: corrupt governments, a lack of available expertise, closed countries and religious walls, to name just a few. And we fight against principalities and powers—a present darkness fueled by the evil one who wants to destroy people's life. But none of these is an excuse for the Christian community to continue to live without compassion.

Moreover, we should never underestimate the impact that this kind of engagement would have on the evangelistic mission of the church. Our deeds of service can create an openness to the message of the good news of Jesus. What gains begrudging respect from those who want to reject and even hate the Christian message are undeniable acts of compassion in the name of Christ.

Take Nicholas Kristoff as an example. Kristoff is a *New York Times* editorial writer who, in his own words, "disagrees strongly with most evangelical Christians, theologically and politically." Yet he wrote an editorial about evangelical Christian work, particularly in Mozambique, titled "God on Their Side." In it he recounts the story of how a seventeen-year-old named Sonia Angeline was rescued from the town garbage dump while enduring four days of labor pains. She didn't have the money to take a taxi to the hospital and was a hair's breadth from dying during childbirth when Katrin Blackert, a twenty-three-year-old volunteer with Iris Ministries, encountered her on her regular visits to children in the camp. Blackert paid for the cab and saved Sonia Angeline's life. After observing the kind of ministry that was taking place, Kristoff was forced to conclude, "But I'm convinced that we should celebrate the big evangelical push into Africa because the bottom line is that it will mean more orphanages, more schools, and above all, more clinics and hospitals."[6]

There is no argument against compassion. The world will take notice. Where will you reveal the compassionate Christ who comes alongside human brokenness?

THE ESSENTIAL COMMANDMENT IN SUMMARY

We are called to connect head and heart, faith and works, love for God and love for our neighbor. Jesus' words in the Essential Commandment take us to the very core of what this life is about for the days we have on this planet. He tells us to be laser-focused on continuous growth in loving Him "with all [our] heart and with all [our] soul and with all [our] mind and with all [our] strength" so that we can love our neighbor who is in need of mercy, and even our enemies. Remember, Jesus wouldn't call us to this if it were not possible; through his empowering grace we can continuously grow in our ability to do so. He believes in you and me.

---

[1]Not her real name.

[2]Os Guinness, *The Dust of Death* (Downers Grove, Ill.: InterVarsity Press, 1973), p. 385.

[3]Richard Stearns, *The Hole in Our Gospel* (Nashville: Thomas Nelson, 2010), p. 216.

[4]Ibid., p. 218.

[5]Ibid., p. 219.

[6]Nicholas Kristoff, *New York Times* editorial, September 27, 2003.

Reading Study Guide

1. According to the reading, compassion is a blend of sympathy and outrage. Within the life of Jesus, how would you summarize what each of these is about?

   a. sympathy:

   b. outrage:

2. Why is sympathy incomplete without outrage, and vice versa?

3. Where does the compassion of Christ in you intersect the brokenness of people's lives?

4. Is there a place of personal pain in your life experience that God might be calling you to turn into a ministry?

   What might that look like?

5. This chapter ends with the challenge that Richard Stearns puts before the church of Christ in his book, *The Hole in Our Gospel*. In what way does Stearns challenge your financial commitment to works of compassion?

6. How is your imagination captured when you think of the potential impact that the Christian church can have on human need?

7. How do you think acts of service help people "hear" the message of the gospel?

8. We began this study with the idea that Jesus actually thinks it is possible to live into the Essential Commandment. How does Jesus' actual belief in you spur you on in your passion to live out this commandment?

Going Deeper

Foster, Richard. *Streams of Living Water: Celebrating the Great Traditions of Christian Faith.* San Francisco: HarperSanFrancisco, 1998. Foster identifies social justice as one of the six streams that represent the totality of the gospel, dedicating chapter five to the topic. His descriptive line for this stream is "Discovering the Compassionate Life." He both develops the biblical concept of justice and shows from history how Christians have been at the forefront of reform in matters such as civil rights, the exploitation of the poor and more. The passion reflected in James's declaration that "faith by itself . . . is dead. . . . I will show you my faith by what I do" (James 2:17-18) is clearly illustrated in Foster's chapter as well.

Appendix A

HOW ARE WE TO UNDERSTAND
THE ESSENTIAL COMMANDMENT?

The following brief description captures the working model that serves as the structure of this book and offers a way to understand the interior structure of human beings as delineated by Jesus in the Essential Commandment.

Since Jesus commands us to love God with all of our heart, soul, mind and strength, aren't we to understand these as the components that make up our individuality? We often pass over these elements without seeing them as a description of our makeup as human beings, concluding that Jesus is simply telling us to "love God with all you've got with supreme devotion." In repeating the phrase "with all your" for each of these four aspects, though, Jesus seems to be drawing attention to them; the structure of his command implies that there is something we can do in regard to each of these aspects (heart, soul, mind, strength) of our makeup. I believe we are to deploy each one in service to God with the utmost devotion.

It has been much debated in theological circles which constituent parts make up a human life. What truly constitutes a human being? What are the core elements needed for "personhood"? This question seems to lead us first to the second constituent part mentioned in Jesus' command—the soul. The way we understand the soul opens up our understanding of the nature of human life. Most discussions on the soul, however, leave me with a vague and rather nebulous impression that's too illusive for me to get my mind around; defining and understanding the soul can be like nailing the proverbial JELL-O to a tree.

Though the usage of the word *soul* is quite varied, the dominant sense from the Scripture is that the soul is equated with personhood. With that in mind, here is how I visualize or put together Jesus' understanding of the nature of personhood (life or *psyche*) as he laid it out in the Essential Commandment.

Every person is a soul made up of three highly interactive, inseparable component parts: heart, mind and body. As Dallas Willard says, the soul "correlates, integrates, and enlivens the various dimensions of the self."[1]

The Scripture tells us that all human beings are souls, and as soulful beings, each of us is being formed spiritually. The state of the soul, however, depends on whether we are in rebellion against God or have been penetrated by the life of God, whether we are moving away from God or toward God.

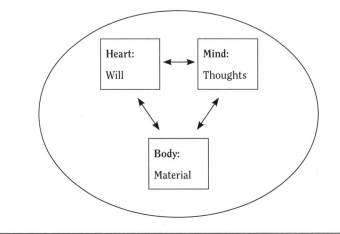

Figure A.1. The *natural* soulful person

Paul gives us a picture of the *natural* person—someone who does not understand the things of God (1 Corinthians 2:14). These people believe the gospel is foolishness, and their souls have settled for far less than the satisfaction that only the one true God offers; though God places eternity in our hearts, many live only for what time offers. Idols made by humans have become the object of their devotion. The souls in rebellion against God are not on God's wavelength; they are tuned to a frequency that makes them deaf to God's invitation. The soul without God is dead to the things of God.

Some souls, however, have been imbued with the life of Spirit.

The difference between the natural and the spiritual person is a life that comes from outside and penetrates the individual. Jesus told Nicodemus that he had to be born from above or born again (John 3:3). What he meant by this is that there is a life force which does

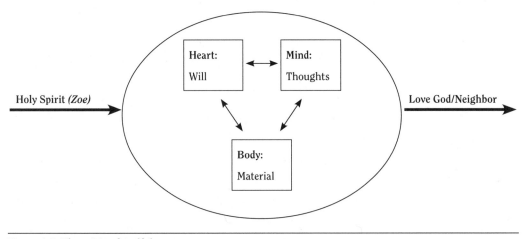

Figure A.2. The *spiritual* soulful person

not exist in the natural person. The word used almost exclusively in the Gospels for this life force is *zoe*. This life force is what Jesus is talking about in John 10:10, for example, where he says, "I have come that they may have life *[zoe]*, and have it to the full." The most well-known verse in Scripture also uses *zoe:* "For God so loved the world that he gave his one and only Son, that whoever believes in him shall not perish but have eternal life *[zoe]*" (John 3:16).

There is just one of two trajectories for us as soulful beings, then: we're either a soulful (natural) person who is moving away from God or a soulful (spiritual) person who is moving toward God or who has been penetrated by *zoe*.

We are each a soulful being, made up of heart, mind and body. And, because we're soulful beings, each of us is being formed spiritually. When Jesus says, "Love the Lord your God with all your heart and with all your soul and with all your mind and with all your strength" and "love your neighbor as yourself," he is assuming that we have caught the infection of *zoe*. Only if this good infection has penetrated our life can we be transformed into the person God intends for us to be.[2] As soulful beings, the heart, mind and body are each to be transformed intentionally and interactively so that we can love God and one another in an *agape* fashion. So though we will look at each of the elements and attempt to get to their core so they can be deployed fully in pursuit of our highest vocation, we need to keep in mind that they ultimately interface with each other inseparably in ways that we can never fully explain. The heart, mind and body comprise our life (soulfulness) as they blend together and influence each other.

---

[1]Dallas Willard, *Renovation of the Heart* (Colorado Springs: NavPress, 2002), p. 199.
[2]C. S. Lewis, *Mere Christianity* (New York: Macmillan, 1943).

Discussion Guide

1. How are we to understand the relationship between the soul and the other constituent parts of a human being?

2. What is the difference between a natural soulful person and a spiritual soulful person?

3. What relationship between heart, mind and body does the figure indicate?

Appendix B

BUILDING A DISCIPLESHIP MINISTRY

My vision is to see disciples made and churches empowered through the multiplication of small, reproducible discipleship groups. It has been my joy as a pastor to witness the transformation of churches through this expanding network, and to receive continuous reports about the value of this approach in implementing a strategy of disciplemaking.

After years of trial and error in attempting to disciple others, I have arrived at the following five criteria as essential to any program of discipleship. These criteria then serve as the basis upon which this tool has been designed.

LIFE INVESTMENT

Discipling is not a six-week program. We are geared to herding people in mass through a program, and once completed, we expect mature disciples to pop out at the other end. Classroom models are necessarily focused on mastering content at the same pace for all, with standardized requirements. Disciplemaking should be viewed in terms of a parent's investment in a child who is nurtured through the stages of infancy, childhood, adolescence and finally into adulthood. Making disciples will only occur when we change our thinking from a quick fix to a long-term life investment. In the long run the results are both deeper and numerically greater.

It may be three to five years before the effects of this approach on the quality and vitality of a church will be seen. Those selected for leadership of the church will be those who have been discipled and in turn can disciple others. The leadership base will be expanded, and spontaneous ministry will begin as "self-starters" energize the body of Christ. Mission groups will crop up because qualified leaders have a passion to meet a heart-felt need.

TRANSFERABILITY

In my discipling efforts I had been frustrated by my inability to move the discipling process beyond the first generation. Those in whom I had invested either did not catch the vision or did not feel equipped to do for others what I had been attempting to do for them. Yet, inherent in anything called discipling must be the ability to transfer life to life to life. When Paul wrote Timothy, he looked four generations down the road (2 Timothy 2:2).

One of the obstacles to transferability is dependency. In a one-to-one relationship an authoritarian model of discipler over disciple can lead to an unhealthy reliance upon the "mature" believer. This is especially true when pastors disciple "laity." For transferability to occur one must move out of a hierarchical view to one of mutual dependency or inter-dependence. Instead of parent-child, teacher-student images for discipleship, I much prefer a relational model of partners walking together toward maturity in Christ. The discipler in this process is not so much a teacher as a guide, facilitator or partner along the way.

From the beginning of the discipling relationship, the new disciple is asked to give serious consideration to continuing the discipling chain by committing to the next generation. The process of weaning disciples away from the discipler is supported by sharing the leadership of the discipleship sessions among the group members. This allows disciples to practice in a safe environment what they will be asked to do in their next discipleship unit.

PURPOSEFULNESS

Spiritual maturity is difficult to quantify. However, if disciplines are being practiced, if content is being learned and applied, and if lifestyle changes are taking place, then progress is experienced. For example, Paul apparently felt mature disciples should know their spiritual gifts and be using them. They also should be reproducing themselves in the next generation. This approach to discipling is designed to give participants a sense of growth toward maturity.

I do not mean to imply that if you master this content, you automatically become a mature disciple, as if it is the tool that transforms. But entering the discipline of this process creates a context for the Holy Spirit to do his work.

FLEXIBILITY

If you are discipling more than one group at a time, there is a need to be at a different point with each. Discipling is by design individualized instruction. There is content to be absorbed, there are tools to be practiced, and there are personal lifestyle changes to be made. No two people do this in the same way or at the same speed. Therefore an approach to discipling will take into account that Christ is formed in each person on a timetable unique to each of them.

This can put a strain on disciplers who are investing themselves in a number of people who are at very different points of spiritual development. One of the advantages of *The Essential Commandment* is the sequential nature of the teaching design. This means you can be studying a different chapter with each person you are discipling. You can go as fast or as slow as needed, without worrying that you are at the same point with each person.

PREPARATION

Once you get into a multiple discipling situation, the time you will have to prepare for each appointment will be limited. This is especially true if the discipler is a pastor. Given the preparation for weekly teaching and preaching events, a pastor will have neither the time nor the emotional energy to prepare two or three different lessons a week for discipling.

The Essential Commandment is a tool which disciplers can use to convey their vast experience and knowledge. The core truth brings to focus their life experience and theological training. Initially, preparation time is required for the discipler to master the lessons, but once the lessons are mastered the material can be used in multiple discipling appointments with a minimum of preparation. Since the format is so simple, the only preparation needed to cover the same material with other disciples is a brief review along with prayer for the disciples.

May we be empowered to do God's work in God's way so that the whole world may know the good news of Jesus Christ.

FOR FURTHER TRAINING

In order to pass on the vision and skills necessary for a church- or ministry-based discipleship strategy, I have developed a five-hour training workshop. I am available on request to train your leaders in the criteria and methods for a discipleship program. I can be reached at the following:

email: gregogden15@gmail.com
website: www.gregogden.com

—Greg Ogden

ALSO AVAILABLE

Discipleship Essentials
Greg Ogden

978-0-8308-1087-1, paperback, 237 pages

Leadership Essentials
Greg Ogden and Daniel Meyer

978-0-8308-1097-0, paperback, 176 pages

Witness Essentials
Daniel Meyer

Available March 2012

978-0-8308-1089-5, paperback, 208 pages